M000214835

IDLER BOOKS

An Idler's Manual

Tom Hodgkinson is editor of the *Idler* magazine and author of several books including *How to Be Idle*, *How to Be Free*, *The Idle Parent* and *Business for Bohemians*. He lives in London. Sign up for his free newsletter at idler.co.uk.

How to Be Idle
How to Be Free
The Idle Parent
The Book of Idle Pleasures (*with Dan Kieran*)
The Ukulele Handbook (*with Gavin Pretor-Pinney*)
Business for Bohemians
How to Live in the Country

AN IDLER'S MANUAL

Tom Hodgkinson

with illustrations by
Alice Smith

IDLER BOOKS

MMXXI

First published in 2021
by Idler Books

Great Western Studios,
65 Alfred Road
London W2 5EU

ISBN 978-1-901170-34-4

FIRST EDITION

Typesetting by Bracketpress

Printed and bound in the UK by
Paragon Customer Commincations

In memory of Cat Ledger (1957–2020)

*The soul in which philosophy dwells
should by its health make even the body healthy.
It should make its tranquillity and gladness shine out
from within; should form in its own mould the outward
demeanour, and consequently arm it with a graceful pride,
an active and joyous bearing, and a contented and
good-natured countenance. The surest sign of
wisdom is constant cheerfulness.*
Montaigne

Contents

Introduction   xi

1. Read ancient philosophy   1
2. Keep a diary   11
3. Stare at a wall   16
4. Get a bicycle   23
5. Make sandwiches   27
6. Stay in bed   31
7. Ponder the animals   35
8. Make a shed   39
9. Play ukulele   44
10. Wander the city   48
11. Make a herb garden   51
12. Get out into the woods (or parks)   54
13. Chuck the smartphone   58
14. Be near water   62
15. Sit on a public bench   65
16. Seek an altered state   67

17. Take a tea break
    (and a lunch break and a coffee break) 74

18. Lie down   76

19. Throw a feast   80

20. Play old games   85

21. Take a day off   88

22. Remove yourself from social media   94

23. Avoid travel   99

24. Loll by the fire   104

    Epilogue   107

    Acknowledgements   109

Introduction

I N AUGUST 1993, following a short delay caused by a particularly gripping Wimbledon tennis tournament, my friend Gav and I published issue one of the *Idler* magazine. It had a decidedly uncommercial cover: a painting of an old white guy in a wig.

The *Idler*'s mission was to change the meaning of the word "idle". We wanted it to be seen as a positive, not a pejorative. We wanted to tell the world that idling is good for you, to restore nobility to the fine art of doing nothing.

Our cover star, the melancholy and humane Dr Johnson, had written in defence of idling as a creative tool. To be creative, he said, you need the time to think, ponder, reflect. And he defined idling as an aspiration, writing, "Every man is, or hopes to be, an idler."

Media reaction was mixed. "It's good but editor young Tom Hodgkinson, 25, will need imagination to keep the joke going," said the *Daily Telegraph*. And *Private Eye* called the *Idler* "a one-joke fanzine".

Growth was to be leisurely. A couple of years after we launched, a mail-order book-delivery company started. In the office, we scoffed. "It's turning over less than a corner shop!" Its name was Amazon, and from supposedly humble

– though clearly arrogant – roots, it has since grown into the biggest company in the world and employs over a million people, while in the same time the *Idler* has grown from a staff of two, to a staff of three, then four, then back to two, then one, then two then four, then two again. Our humble roots remain very much in evidence.

Still, what's the hurry? Do I want to make billions and go into space? No. Help people live the #idlelife? Yes.

And the *Idler*, though possibly under-staffed, has helped thousands of people to live more satisfying and fulfilling lives through our magazine, website, events and our online courses, as well as my own series of radical lifestyle manifestos, which began with *How to Be Idle* in 2004.

For five years my partner Victoria Hull and I ran a school, café and bookshop in west London. We called it the Idler Academy of Philosophy, Husbandry and Merriment. The idea was to teach those three curricular pillars, and to promote our values of learning and conviviality.

In that time many thousands of people came through our doors to take a course, listen to a talk, buy a book or just hang out and do nothing.

The bricks-and-mortar shop has evolved into our online Academy, where we bring you our favourite teachers and generally inspiring humans. And through our weekly "Drink with the Idler" online events, we introduce you to subversive thinkers, merry souls, brilliant artists and free spirits.

What we aim to bring you is freedom, fun and a joyful grabbing hold of life, in a world where jobs, governments, bureaucracies and money-lenders can hold us back from living the lives we want to lead.

The *Idler* will help you to free your spirit, expand your mind and have a lot of fun in the process. Our philosophy is broadly Epicurean (of which more in these pages): you'll banish anxiety and revolutionise your everyday life.

This book is a manual. That word derives from *manus*, the Latin for hand, and in ancient and medieval times referred to a book small enough to be held in the hand. "Handbook" would be another translation. The manuals were originally produced by the Greek philosophers, and later by priests.

The book you hold offers you 24 practical ideas on how to bring some idling – and therefore some real quality and fun – into your life.

Join me as we explore various tips, tricks and ideas to help you create the life you want to lead: the good life, the philosophical life, the romantic life, the fun life – in short, the idle life.

Tom Hodgkinson
August 2021

1

Read ancient philosophy

When will I be free
To breathe the delightful forgetfulness of life's cares,
Among ancient classics, with sleep and idle hours?
Horace

THE PHILOSOPHERS OF ANCIENT Athens were the original idlers. The very word "philosopher" actually suggested something of a lack of ambition. It doesn't mean "wise person"; more "someone who would like to be wise, but isn't yet". The literal meaning is "lover of wisdom". And they really can help us all to find happiness.

The philosophers, of whom Socrates was really the first, set themselves up in opposition to a group of teachers in Greece called the Sophists. The word means "wise ones" (we might call them know-it-alls) and they were a bunch of chancers who set themselves up as tutors to the ambitious male youth of the day and made a lot of money doing so. Actually the philosophers often had pretty good relationships with the Sophists, and one of Plato's dialogues features one, Protagoras, who seems perfectly all right.

But the Greek philosophers were altogether more laid

back, were less money-focused and certainly had more humility and better beards. For Socrates, at least as he is presented in Plato's lovely dialogue *The Symposium*, philosophy was a sort of moving towards; it was a longing, a love. You know how in Spanish, when you say you love someone, you say *Te quiero*? It means "I want you", but I don't have you.

So philosophy means both a lack of and a love for wisdom. So, said Socrates, to be a philosopher is to admit that you're in love with wisdom, and also that you have not yet won her. In a sense, you're still at the stalking stage. You are a troubadour, a courtier, a paramour, a wooing lover.

The philosophers were also pretty monklike and could be seen as the ancestors of medieval monks. Plato invented the monastery in the form of his Academy, a resort for reflection which survived for 600 years. The Greek philosophers dressed in simple clothes, grew long beards and wandered around holding a staff. They rejected the rat race.

These would all seem to us to be fairly harmless ideas, but Socrates was put to death by the Athenian state for promoting them. Before he drank the hemlock that would kill him, by gradually poisoning his body from the feet up, he told his followers he didn't care and in fact was looking forward to dying, as he would finally become a free-floating soul without a body, soul-consciousness being one of the aims of philosophy. A cheerful soul.

Socrates, then, was a Christ-like figure who has inspired millions to make efforts to take some control over their lives and try to find both freedom and peace. Following his death, various schools of philosophy appeared. His student and number-one fan, Plato, started the Academy and attempted to use the intellect to grapple with the problems of being alive.

A second school inspired by Socrates was the Stoic one, founded by Zeno of Citium. They believed in some sort of cosmic path or direction. If you could go with the flow, then you would become unruffled. The slings and arrows would not perturb you, because of your fundamental belief in fate. Everything has a reason. The Roman Stoic philosopher Epictetus, advised people to control the things that were in their power, and not to stress about the things that weren't in their power. Being "philosophical" about problems in life is being Stoic.

There were the Sceptics who took Socrates's famous phrase "I know nothing" and spun it into a philosophy that revolved around asking questions.

The Cynics, led by Diogenes, picked up on Socrates's rejection of customs like wearing fine clothes and making money. They dressed in rags, spat at the rich, masturbated in public and rejected the consumer society. They were the punks of ancient Athens.

Diogenes the Cynic was the son of a banker. In a well-known piece of performance art, he lived for a while in a wine cask which he placed by the cathedral wall. The word "cynic" or *kynikos* literally means "doglike", because it was said that Cynics lived like dogs: homeless, jobless and clothesless – but always cheerful. From *kynikos* is derived our word "canine", meaning that in Blighty we ought to call the Cynics "the Canines".

Then there was Aristotle's school of reasonableness. He studied with Plato at the Academy for 20 years and then broke off to start his own school, the Lyceum. He was all about balance and moderation. Nothing to extremes. He agreed with Socrates that we should all make time for philosophy, for studying the arts of living well. But he didn't think you should quit your job and retreat from the world. You should work to buy the time for leisure – during which you should educate yourself.

The Greek word *schole*, from which we get "school", meant leisure. Leisure, to the philosophers, was a greater treasure than work or money-getting. Leisure time was the greatest luxury. The more leisure time you had, in their view, the more successful you were.

It was with these thoughts in mind that we at the Idler Academy crafted our Latin epigram – *libertas per cultum* – meaning freedom through education.

None of the ancient schools reckoned that work was at the heart of meaning and fulfilment for human beings. That pernicious myth came much later as capitalism first began to get established during the Reformation and then developed under the Protestants of the 17th and 18th centuries, and accelerated during the Industrial Revolution.

Perhaps the most relevant of the great Greek schools as far as idling goes was the Epicurean one, founded by the guru Epicurus. Epicurus never once mentions work in his writings. His aim was to help people to find *ataraxia*, which we would translate as peace or undisturbedness.

To do this, he retreated from city life and bought a house just outside Athens which he called the Garden. He gathered around him a group of followers, who included friends, couples, courtesans and a slave called Mouse. Today we'd call it an intentional community. The group lived here for 35 years and kick-started a philosophical movement which lives to this day. We tend to think of "Epicurean" as a synonym for luxurious living but in fact it means almost the opposite. Epicurus prided himself on his frugality and boasted he could live on a copper coin a day. He avoided wine and was just as happy with bread and water as with a feast.

However, the Epicureans did seek pleasure and avoid pain. The inscription above the entrance to Epicurus's Garden supposedly read:

Stranger, your time will be pleasant here. Here the highest good is pleasure.

Epicurus was a materialist. He believed in the theory of atoms which had been developed by an earlier thinker, Democritus. He felt that much anxiety was caused by an irrational belief in portents, spells, magic, consumerism and hocus-pocus. If he could free the people of their absurd, groundless, superstitious or vain beliefs, then the anxiety would be lifted. He maintained there was no life after death and that the world consisted simply of atoms and void.

In Epicurus, you get no "vain fantasies of Providence" – as Karl Marx put it in his 1842 doctoral thesis, "The Difference Between the Democritean and Epicurean Philosophy of Nature", clearly an attack on the Stoic notion of the *logos*. The first step to freedom was to discard the mumbo-jumbo and see the world clearly, and this philosophy clearly led directly to Marx's materialism and famous statement "Religion is the opium of the people" – an aphorism that could have been written by the anti-religious Epicurus.

Epicurus's innovation spawned a veritable movement, and 300 years later, the Roman lawyer and philosopher Cicero, who was a fan, commented on the Epicurean craze, saying, "They have taken over all of Italy." You could compare its popularity among the well-heeled of Rome to today's mindfulness craze. Then as now, the busy and successful classes were keen to show off their other, more philosophical side, and to take a rest from anxiety, and so the Romans built Epicurean retreats and created libraries of Epicurean books. To take one well-known example, Virgil lived on an Epicurean commune in Naples and wrote his bucolic poems there. The Georgics are dedicated to Siro, the Epicurean teacher guru who led the community. There have been many mediocre Stoic writers but it took an Epicurean to create something truly great.

Now though they were against organised religion, the

Epicureans did believe in some sort of higher power or gods. Epicurus told his fellow Greeks that the popular gods, the capricious characters of myth, didn't exist. He thought that they were absurd fabrications, much as Protestant reformers felt that saints and miracles and purgatory were vain superstitions which kept the people in a state of fear and led them to hand over money to unscrupulous clerics.

Epicurus's gods were completely inactive. They existed to show us the way. They were paragons of the good life. He imagined gods as idle entities, who sat around on clouds doing precisely nothing. It was their example that we should follow. The more inactive the better. In this the gods of Epicurus were nothing like the flawed and overly active gods of the Roman imagination. Epicurus reckons that enlightenment will lead to a vision of these idle gods:

> As soon as the voice of reason rises from your godlike mind to enunciate the nature of things, the terror in the soul dissolves, the walls of the world fall back, and I see what comes to pass throughout the void. The holy godheads are manifested, and their tranquil thrones; the winds do not buffet them or clouds bestrew them with storms, nor snow, clotted by piercing frost, profane them with falling hoar.

Well, that's always been such a problem for me – getting constantly profaned with falling hoar; God it's annoying.

Epicurean scholar George K Strodach reckons that these deities are wholly idle: "Their perfection and self-involvement absolved them from doing anything – from motion and activity of any sort, and from the duties and responsibilities that deities would normally have, such as the creation and supervisioning of the world."

The gods of Epicurus, then, are gloriously lazy and we should follow their example, and laze about under the greenwood tree with a lover. Shakespeare imagined this scene in *As You Like It* in a very Epicurean poem, which clearly went on to influence the life of Baloo the bear in *The Jungle Book*, who tells us to forget about our trouble and our strife:

> *Under the greenwood tree*
> *Who loves to lie with me,*
> *And turn his merry note*
> *Unto the sweet bird's throat;*
> *Come hither, come hither, come hither;*
> *Here he shall see*
> *No enemy*
> *But winter and rough weather.*
>
> *Who doth ambition shun*
> *And loves to live i' the sun,*
> *Seeking the food he eats*
> *And pleas'd with what he gets,*
> *Come hither, come hither, come hither:*
> *Here he shall see*
> *No enemy*
> *But winter and rough weather.*

Baloo, we might note, in the original book, counsels Mowgli to "think and be still", in other words, to be idle.

Epicurus has another practical tip for avoiding anxiety, and that is to shun the political life. He shares this opinion with today's non-voting anarchists: when you stop acting as a political animal, they argue, you start to take responsibility for your own life, because you are no longer waiting for others to sort it out for you.

Having passed through a Stoic phase, I would now say that Stoicism is far too harsh a philosophy for everyday use. It is also mumbo-jumbo. The Stoic teachers say that everything has a meaning and a purpose and they say you should not be upset if your daughter dies. Which is kind of, er, harsh.

Epicureanism is the way. Enjoying pleasure but being happy with what you have.

So that's my first tip. Read about and read the old books of philosophy. The act of reading itself is a form of idling. Read slowly, drift off and be with Keats who advised people not to try to understand everything, and to enjoy, in a sense, being in a muddle, to enjoy being a philosopher.

Inaction points

☞ Read *The Art of Happiness* by Epicurus, in the Penguin Classics edition. Keep it by the bed, dip into it, savour the ideas.

☞ Read *The Symposium* by Plato. There is a nice unstuffy translation out there by Shelley, but any will do. It's the story of a boozy dinner party attended by some of ancient Athens's finest: Aristophanes, Alcibiades and others, and the source of ideas about "Platonic love", and the origin of the word "philosophy" as revealed to Socrates by his teacher, the priestess Diotima. Just read a few lines at a time, let them swill around in your brain, and don't worry if the meaning is not clear.

☞ Read *The Manual* by Epictetus to get the Stoic view.

☞ Read *Lives of the Philosophers* by Diogenes Laertius.

☞ Read bits of the above out loud to each other in the evening or while on a picnic. Reading out loud is, again, an ancient and enjoyable (and free) idle pursuit.

2
Keep a diary

*The act of diary writing is a defiance, a defence of the
personal and the private in an increasingly automated,
encrypted, algorithmically organised world.*
Michael Palin

ONE OF THE MANY great achievements of the charming
Python Michael Palin is his diary. Since 1958, he has kept
a diary almost every day. He says it's a "daily verbal and
mental workout which I could not now do without".

As someone who has always tried and always failed to
keep a diary, I wanted advice on how to do it, so I asked
Palin to write a guide to diary-writing for the *Idler* magazine. I was after the practicalities: when he writes it, where,
how often, with what sort of notebook. (If you want advice
on something, always find someone with proven success in
that area to help you.)

The piece Palin wrote demonstrated a principle of idling:
routine and habit help enormously. This may sound
counter-intuitive. Surely idling is about doing what you
feel? No, because if you do not schedule your idling, you
will be easy prey for the attention merchants out there, the

Silicon Valley platforms and scams, the advertising people, the distractors, who spend vast sums employing behavioural scientists to get you to hang around on their sites, clicking and spending. In scheduling is freedom.

I followed Palin's advice and I can report that it works. I am now in the habit of writing in my diary every day. Each morning before starting work, I sit down with a pen and notebook and write up events of the previous day. It takes about ten or 15 minutes.

Here, for you, I reproduce Palin's key bits of advice:

Try to write your diary at the same time each day. This way it more easily becomes what it should be – a part of your everyday life. I write mine at my desk, before I start work at 9am. I tried writing on the evening of the same day, but couldn't read my writing for wine splodges.

Choose the right equipment. I prefer to write in a good stout hardcover notebook. It gives the diary some consequence – a feeling of substance – and also more of a chance of survival.

I write my entries longhand and will continue to do so. I worry that handwriting is fast becoming an endangered art. And it's a sensual thing. I like the feeling of contact between the pen I'm holding and the paper I'm writing on. I kid myself that it makes the thoughts flow better. And it makes the act of diary-writing different from the emails and keyboards on which I conduct my daily business.

This last is an important point. In diaries is idleness. Writing a diary injects a period of solitary reflection into your day, a bit of me time, to use the phrase loved by women's magazines, and a precious few moments also freed from the siren strains of Silicon Valley.

Let me add that diary-keeping is wonderfully therapeutic. It's like having a shrink. The very act of writing down what's been happening helps you to process your life and to look at it from the outside – a technique for happiness that Stoics as well as shrinks recommend.

And how much emotion and judgement do you put into your diary? My friend Rachael Hunt asked me what I wrote in it. I said, "Oh just the facts, you know – 'another tedious evening at the Hunts'."

Your journal does not need to contain only a record of what you did yesterday. You can use it in many other ways. George Orwell used to paste cuttings into his journal. I often get a tube of Pritt Stick and stick a receipt or train ticket in my diary. Such ephemera might look boring today – but imagine inspecting them in ten or 50 years' time.

Your diary can also be used as a notebook or sketchbook or indeed commonplace book. Idler Academy writing teacher John-Paul Flintoff recommends doing this: keeping a commonplace book is a tradition that has sadly more or less died. It just means keeping a notebook into which you copy bits of other people's writing that you like. This manual you are reading now has elements of a commonplace book: I am using it to share with you bits of writing I like. I hope you will share my enthusiasm.

Flintoff loves the actual process of copying out passages from other writers by hand. He finds this helps enormously with his own writing. And, he says, copying is a time-honoured technique:

> As a young man, Hunter S Thompson typed out *The Great Gatsby* – the entire book. In fact, he did it more than once – because he wanted to know what it felt like to write a masterpiece. A hundred years earlier, practically every writer did something similar – gathering verbal wonders in a "commonplace book", to play around with, and rehash in their own work. One who did that was George Eliot, whose commonplacing I inspected at the British Library.

Commonplacing, as it was called, used to be customary, and some of these books – eccentric anthologies, you could call them – were published. One lovely example is *The Knapsack*, a commonplace book assembled by the art critic Herbert Read (1893–1968). It's 600 pages of poetry, prose, fiction and essays. It was designed for soldiers and is a lovely companion for anyone. I keep a copy by the bedside and pop it in my overnight bag when going on a short trip.

Your journal can also be used for sketching. Follow David Hockney's advice and just draw whatever happens to be in front of you. Sketch a flower, a book, a lamp. Again, the act of sketching injects idling and reflection into your day. And at the end of it, you have created something. Your soul has been fed.

And of course there is the ancient idler's pursuit of doodling. Doodling is the unmediated musings of the soul on paper.

A diary or journal is an aid to reflection, to creative thought, to the care of your soul. Every idler should have one.

Inaction points

☞ Buy a nice notebook. I use Europe Notemakers, ring-bound exercise books with nice bright covers. Sit down each morning for ten or 15 minutes and write a short account of the events of the previous day. Repeat. Stick to the facts. Don't worry if you miss a day. You can catch up with a brief entry later. As time goes on, carry out literary experiments in your diary. Record dialogue, paint scenes, doodle, sketch.

3
Stare at a wall

Along the way, Socrates begins to lag behind, and he waves
his friend onward. Upon arriving at the house, he takes up
a post at the neighbour's porch, and stands meditating.
Plato, *The Symposium*

THIS IS A VERY straightforward form of meditation, or idling, and one I practise a few times every day. It's easy to find a wall: I have a wall in my backyard, and there are loads of them in the house. In the evening I sit on a bench and stare at the wall, alone, almost always with a bottle of Doom Bar, a fine ale from Cornwall. In the morning, before rising, I lie in bed, propped up on a few pillows, and stare at the bedroom wall.

And I don't call it mindfulness. I call it meditation. But what is meditation? Well, it is not simply a stress coping strategy or a method of focusing. In the West, that is what it has become through its secular offshoot, mindfulness. The mindfulness craze has taken a millennia-old spiritual practice, designed to unify us with a higher power or universal consciousness, and turned it into a means of getting ahead in the workplace.

When you hear that tech bro Jack Dorsey, the CEO of an ad sales business called Twitter, does mindfulness each morning for half an hour, you can be sure that it has degenerated into a money-making technique.

Mindfulness is also used by large corporations as a method of calming its employees and trying to prevent them from having nervous breakdowns brought on by the realisation that they are stuck in a meaningless job which contributes nothing of real value to the world.

Mindfulness now, far from helping us to dissolve into the cosmic oneness of the universe, promises simply to get us ahead in the capitalist system, or to help make profits for the mill owners.

And its practitioners dream up silly apps which we pay for and in the process make themselves piles of cash. One such example is the founder of a computer game called Moshi Monsters. He discovered that making millions from Moshi Monsters had not made him happy, so he decided instead to make millions from selling mindfulness to the stressed-out masses via mobile phones, and this seems to have done the trick.

Sometimes, I might add, you don't need a mindfulness app. You need to quit your job and do something you enjoy instead.

And as for what meditation actually is, I have some history in this department. When I was 13 my father joined an Indian spiritual organisation called the Brahma Kumaris or BKs. They're a women-led group with several hundred centres around the world. They practise a form of yoga called Raja Yoga. This resulted in my dad renouncing sex, meat and ambition and getting up at four in the morning and meditating.

I asked the BKs' European director, Sister Jayanti, how she would define meditation. She was very clear that it's about connecting with your soul or spirit, away from the ego, and not simply a way of coping with stress.

> Meditation is to be able to focus my thoughts in a very specific direction and to focus my thoughts on the awareness of the being I am internally, the spiritual being. And secondly, to be able to connect to the divine. It's these two parts that comprise meditation.
>
> Being calm is actually a side effect of meditation.
>
> Mindfulness has become something that people promote in the secular world in a secular way – for example, to help the corporates, because its teaching focuses attention on the present and allows a person to be more concentrated. If you trace back mindfulness it's connected with the Hindu scriptures, which came from the Buddhist scriptures. The idea originally was that it should be focused on an inner being – but somewhere along the line that got lost.
>
> Meditation will reduce blood pressure, calm the body down, give you greater stamina, help you develop your tolerance capacity for pain or heat or cold – all of that is absolutely a fact – but that's not the purpose of meditation. When you meditate you are connecting to an inner being and finding qualities that are in the

spirit, the soul. Through connecting to the divine you receive an influx of energy and power.

Wall yoga, as I call it, has as good a claim to be a real yoga as the rest of them. And there are many yogas. There follows a brief list of the major yogas and their meanings. Yoga of course means union – union with the spirit, union with the divine.

Bhakti Yoga: the path of devotion, where people perform rituals. This is also called religion.

Hatha Yoga: the path of force. It uses physical exercises and discipline, and is perhaps the best known in the West. This is the form of yoga that says you can find enlightenment by hanging upside down from a tree, or at the very least saluting the sun.

Karma Yoga: where your work is your yoga. Your duties are your yoga. It could be cooking, cleaning, washing, anything. Or it could be fishing.

Buddhi Yoga: where you just need to focus your intellect, forget about everything else.

Gyan Yoga: the path of knowledge. This is the intellectual yoga, which starts from study of the self and from reading the scriptures.

Raja Yoga: the royal yoga. It incorporates within itself the essence of all the other yogas. There's the love and devotion in worship of Bhakti Yoga as well as the understanding of knowledge of Karma Yoga, to be able to do which you must be engaged in the world but still have that connection to yoga.

Bench yoga: which was invented by comedian Arthur Smith, and there's more on the wonders of the bench later in this manual.

My own evening wall yoga practice is great idling time. It's when I just sit and let my mind wander. My morning wall yoga can also be good. The only problem here is that Victoria, my partner, will walk in while I am in a profound reverie and ask me what the password is for Google Drive. You can do wall yoga in the office, or even on the way to a party, as Socrates does in *The Symposium*. It's yoga for people who can't be bothered to do it, to steal a phrase from that peerless wit Geoff Dyer.

Wall yoga does not reject daydreaming. I don't attempt to empty my head. Sometimes I resolve arguments by at last seeing the thing I was arguing about from the other person's point of view. This is a great benefit of meditation. It helps you to avoid. Dadi Janki, the late leader of the BKs, advised people never to fight. In a fight, there is at best one winner, and often two losers (as anyone who has dealt with lawyers will know). Whereas avoid a battle and there is the chance that both parties will win.

During my meditation, I get ideas, I sometimes worry, I remember people I should be sending a letter or email to. I hope it is something like the trancelike state that Socrates goes into just before he arrives at the dinner party in Plato's *Symposium*. Socrates was a meditator and in fact acres of academic print have been devoted to his strange reveries and what we can learn from them.

But I also get the occasional moment of pure joy when I seem to be connected with everything and everything is all right with the world. It's about finding a space within yourself that is calm, a sort of secluded hut in the mind, next to a babbling brook. This is what Yeats's "Lake Isle of Innisfree" is all about. He says he can find the cabin of peace in his mind. Even when standing "on the pavements grey", he writes, "I feel it in the deep heart's core."

Inaction points

☞ Schedule your wall meditation. Find 20 minutes at the start or end of the day and mark it in your calendar.

☞ Let your mind wander. Don't worry about some abstract notion of "emptying your mind" – even the most advanced Zen masters cannot manage that. Be kind
to yourself.

☞ Grab the moment. You can enter a gentle trance while waiting for the bus or for your partner to get ready when leaving the house, in the manner of Socrates.

You'll find that the day will offer you plenty of idle moments, even when you're stuck in a boring job, when you keep an eye out for them.

4
Get a bicycle

Voltaire himself might have invented the bicycle, since it contributes so much to man's welfare and nothing at all to his bane. Beneficial to the health, it emits no harmful fumes and permits only the most decorous speeds. How can a bicycle ever be an implement of harm?

Angela Carter

MY LIFE IMPROVED dramatically when I bought a bicycle.

It was mainly an economy thing. Victoria and I had recently moved back to London from the wilds of Exmoor. Money was tight, so we made a study of our outgoings. The striking discovery was how much we were spending on tube fares and petrol. It was 30 or 40 quid a week.

There was an added inducement to bicycling in that I was now doing no physical exercise whatsoever. I was turning into a couch potato, having been fairly active in the country, chopping logs, digging the soil and so on. Joining a gym was not an option. Why would I spend money to torture myself? So a bicycle seemed to provide a solution to two problems at once.

What I did not do was buy one of those absurd thousand-pound bikes that you see the competitive slaves of London, dressed in Lycra, riding to work and back. It's a shame that cycling in London has been ruined by these extreme commuters, angry huffers and puffers, who spend fortunes on gear and punish themselves so they can shave a few minutes off the journey to the office of their slave-masters, and terrorise the rest of us in the process.

I have seen these lunatics scaring toddlers in Richmond Park on a Sunday.

No. It's a pottering bike for me. I was advised by a bike shop in west London to look for an old Raleigh Chiltern on eBay. I found a nice green men's Chiltern for £99. It was made in 1996. The bike arrived. It is gorgeous and rides beautifully. Or was gorgeous till Victoria borrowed it and had it stolen. I was then lucky enough to find a neighbour selling a no-gears road bike for £70, so I bought that, and have used it daily since.

I cycle slowly as a protest against the speed monsters. I enjoy this hugely. I wait obediently at lights, and study the architecture around me. I freewheel down hills. I imagine myself to be a Cambridge student circa 1931, on my way to a riveting lecture by FR Leavis, rather than some kind of Tour de France wannabe. On my route to our studio in the morning I cycle past the giant Westfield shopping centre, under the Westway where Gypsies' ponies live, past the mansions of Holland Park, down Portobello Road and along the Great Western canal, past the narrowboats with their smoking chimneys and bicycles strapped to the roof.

To know that such health-giving, money-saving bliss is available so cheaply is a wonder indeed. The bicycle is simplicity, it is efficiency, it is freedom.

Cars are planet-killing, people-killing lumps of metal – and buying a car must be one of the most boring tasks known to 21st-century humankind, since you get sucked into a world of pure unadulterated bullshit.

Not long ago we took our green 15-year-old Vauxhall, bought for a mere £1,000 three years ago, to get the driver's window fixed, and the mechanic told us it was a write-off. There was so much wrong with it, he said, that the cost of repairs would be more than the value of the car itself.

Not only that, as a diesel car it would soon be practically illegal in London.

So we were reluctantly exposed to a world of *Auto Trader*, online searches, loans and absurd reviews that say things like "really fun to drive". Is driving really fun? Or is it a myth that has been told again and again by the car industry for the last hundred years through its clever advertising? When it comes to cars, I'm really with Ivan Illich: I prefer the bicycle and would rather not have a car at all. But as we still have three teenagers and a dog, we decided we needed one.

We now had to decide what car to get. Would it be a petrol car, an electric car, a petrol hybrid or a plug-in hybrid? Saloon, hatchback, estate or SUV (whatever that is)? Big or small?

I became briefly obsessed, in a most unenjoyable way. I even found myself sucked into a kind of interior dialogue

– what sort of car would represent me best? Nothing flashy or new, obviously. But not too grotty either. Economical on long journeys. Cheap to maintain. Ecologically sound (surely the most ecologically sound thing would be not to have a car in the first place – but why does no one say that?).

Cars sell themselves as freedom machines, but are in fact the opposite. If you want to be free, get a bike.

Inaction points

☞ Cycle slowly.
☞ Stop at lights.
☞ Ask your local bike shop for advice.
☞ If in a hilly area, consider an electric bike.
☞ Buy a decent lock.

5
Make sandwiches

Send me a small pot of cheese,
so that when I like I may have a feast.
Epicurus in a letter to a friend

IT'S A FACT of life that no one ever regretted making sandwiches.

For in the sandwich is freedom. Freedom from the taste and choice of others. Freedom to choose. For your sandwich, you can use any bread you like and stuff it with whatever you like. Why not make your own?

When considered rationally, buying a sandwich from a commercial operator is an act of financial recklessness. The same sandwich that will cost you a fiver in the high street will cost mere pence to assemble at home.

When opening your sandwich on the train or on the park bench, you will be filled with a sense of satisfaction and will even feel slightly sorry for the poor deluded consumerist folk around you who have forked out astronomical sums on their commercial preparations.

I have a game with myself, which is to keep the cost of my lunch to one pound. This is achieved by making a simple cheese sandwich for lunch, to be accompanied by an apple. In my mind, this is a Ploughman's Lunch of the sort eaten by a medieval peasant resting under a tree with a bottle of beer after a hard morning's ploughing.

My other tactic is to scrape up a few left-overs from the fridge and reassemble them into something edible.

Another frugal tip, allied to sandwich-making, is coffee-avoiding. I very rarely buy coffee in coffee shops. It's absurdly expensive and often disgusting.

And we drink too much of it. If sleep guru Michael Walker is to be believed, coffee after 10am disrupts your sleep. So I have one small black coffee with breakfast, made with a small stove-top espresso-maker and Lavazza coffee, and that's it. One 250g pack, which costs £3, makes at least 30 delicious coffees. That's ten pence each. Three quid for a month of coffee.

I calculate that by making sandwiches and avoiding coffee shops, I save at least £35 a week. Multiplied by 46 working weeks, that would add up to £1,600, enough to buy a bespoke suit and a pair of brogues from Church's, a brilliant artwork or a luxurious week for two in Naples.

Frugality can be fun. It can also be liberating. The actual act of making the sandwich, too, provides a moment of autonomy and creativity in the day. I love the way that despite his ever-growing drugs fortune, Walter White in *Breaking Bad* makes himself a peanut-butter and jam sandwich each morning before going off for a hard day's work in the meth lab with Jessie Pinkman.

Socrates and the Epicureans were clear on this point:

you really don't need that much to be happy. The point is that you need to be free of money worries, not to have a lot of it. So it makes logical sense to reduce your outgoings.

But you might also want to increase your income a bit. Because you really want to avoid relative poverty, certainly when you have a family. Victoria and I went through a painful two years when we worried non-stop about money. Our shop had failed; I had no book deals and virtually no journalism. I was reduced to rather desperately writing anything at all that the *Daily Mail* wanted. We were never going to starve, and we ate well enough, and I managed to afford cheap beer, but we thought about money all the time. It was exhausting. We felt stingy and we took it out on the children. To our rich friends, our frugality looked like meanness.

Now that we have a reasonable income – more than a nurse, less than a doctor – we are very happy. We have enough. We have plenty. It's the middle way.

The life of a Diogenes or a St Francis of Assisi is not for everyone. It's for only the real extreme cases. Though my dad did it. When he discovered meditation and the spiritual path, he gave away all his money and possessions (though not, unfortunately, to me) and embraced a life of poverty when my brother and I left home. He turned Saddhu.

Maybe that's OK if you are alone and have no dependants. But with a family of five, you need some cash.

The powers that be are known for preaching frugality to the lower orders while themselves remaining undistinguished in that regard. Jeff Bezos endorses frugality in his 14 "leadership principles", a sort of inarticulate Ten Commandments for his million retail slaves (sorry, "athletes"). Clearly he is not frugal in his own everyday life, wasting millions on space trips, nor does he want to encourage frugality in his customers, as that would reduce his share price. It's the same with the former UK chancellor, George Osborne. Following several years of telling UK citizens to tighten their belts, reduce spending and be frugal, he embarked on a veritable orgy of money-making, taking jobs with various money-lending scams in a Tony Blair-like effort to line his own nest with ermine and feathers of gold.

I would finally emphasise the oft-repeated point that frugality is good for the planet. Compare the carbon footprint of making your own sandwiches with buying one at Costa, with all its plastic packaging, transport costs and, very possibly, exploitation of the workers who make the sandwiches. Sandwiches save money and save the planet too.

Inaction points

☞ I don't need to tell you how to make a sandwich. Mine tend to be very simple: bread and cheese. But I get proper sourdough and add good pickle. Pack in either a tupperware box or silver foil. Add an apple.

☞ Take the Idler Academy sourdough course.

6
Stay in bed

*If you do lie in bed, be sure you do it without any reason
or justification at all. I do not speak, of course, of the
seriously sick. But if a healthy man lies in bed,
let him do it without a rag of excuse; then
he will get up a healthy man.*

G K Chesterton

MORRISSEY IS NOT exactly flavour of the month. His Brexity views don't go down well with ageing Smiths fans like me. However, I do admit that I enjoyed his recent single, "I Spent the Day in Bed", in which he advises his listeners to spend the day in bed as an act of resistance to late-stage industrial capitalism. "No boss, no bus, no rain, no train," he says, capturing brilliantly that delicious feeling of self-determination that comes over us when we're skiving off.

He's quite right. And not only do bed-lingerers avoid commuting and bosses, they also do absolutely no harm to anyone. Morrissey's point here brings to mind Pascal's famous staying-in quote:

Sometimes, when I set to thinking about the various activities of men, the dangers and troubles which they face at Court, or in war, giving rise to so many quarrels and passions, daring and wicked enterprises and so on, I have often said that the sole cause of man's unhappiness is that he does not know how to stay quietly in his room. A man wealthy enough for man's needs would never leave home to go to sea or besiege some fortress if he knew how to stay at home and enjoy it.

When lockdowns struck, I eagerly sought out the great stay-at-home books like Huysmans's *À Rebours* which is about a wealthy recluse who studs his pet tortoise with precious jewels, and of course *Journey Around My Room* by the beautifully named Xavier Le Maistre, an 18th century aristocrat who, in order to recover from injuries sustained in a duel, found himself in lockdown for 42 days.

As we have all read and may know from personal experience, lockdowns led to a rise in the number of people working from home, often abbreviated to WFH (as well as an extraordinary explosion in the already massive profits of Apple, Facebook, Google and Microsoft).

But we hear less about working from bed.

Surely that's the next step, and in fact the answer to the problems of finding a quiet space away from delivery people and children, where all your needs are in easy reach and you can recline in a posture suitable for creative thought and peaceful reflection. Let us call it WFB, in the modern manner of three-letter abbreviations (aka TLAs).

What's more, with WFB, you can drift off into a hypna-gogic state after lunch without having to move.

Working from bed has a long and noble history. The *Idler*'s patron saint, Dr Johnson, was well known for it. He would lie in bed all morning, sometimes later, reading his favourite book, *The Anatomy of Melancholy* by Robert Burton, or just thinking. Although Johnson tended to beat himself up about this apparent laziness, the bed-time he put in produced the thoughts he would later write down when he finally roused himself to literary activity.

Florence Nightingale famously went to bed in 1857 in her Mayfair home, possibly exhausted by the effort of having invented modern nursing, and stayed there till her death in 1910. She was enormously productive in her prone state and wrote piles of letters, reports and books on nursing. John Lennon loved his bed and famously worked from the Amsterdam Hilton for a week. Proust was clearly bed-ridden, and Paul Bowles (1910–99), darling of the Beatniks and author of *The Sheltering Sky*, worked from his bed in Tangier, his home for 52 years, where he was inter-viewed for the *Idler* by novelist Marcel Theroux in 1993.

But you don't have to be a pop star, a novelist or a pioneer in the treatment of disease to work from bed. Now, while I am of course aware that dustmen, delivery drivers, builders and a very large host of other workers do not have this option, surely an insurance broker, coder or lawyer could spend at least part of the working day reclining on a bank of puffed-up pillows, with laptop, cup of mint tea and a pile of old books close at hand? Why not?

In fact, the newspapers are telling me today that as a result of the pandemic, it will become the norm to work three days a week from home, and two in the office. This is exactly the kind of future I prayed for when I started the *Idler*. As my friend the organic-food pioneer and giver of macrobiotic food to John and Yoko, Craig Sams, wrote to me, "It's taken a virus just a few months to achieve what you have been toiling away at for years."

This is great news: it means more autonomy, less commuting, less energy expenditure and more working from bed and staying in bed.

Bed means ideas. Bed means creative thought. As the great G K Chesterton wrote in his essay in praise of lying in bed, "I am certain that it was from persons in my position that all the original inspiration came for covering the ceilings of palaces and cathedrals with a riot of fallen angels or victorious gods."

Inaction points
☞ Look at your calendar. Choose a day to stay in bed sometime soon. Write in your calendar, "Bed day". Give yourself that day.
☞ Get up one hour later than normal.
☞ Cast off guilt. Staying in bed is good for you and good for the planet.

7
Ponder the animals

Behold the birds of the heaven, that they sow not, neither do they reap, nor gather into barns; and your heavenly Father feedeth them. Are not ye of much more value than they? And which of you by being anxious can add one cubit unto the measure of his life?
Matthew 6:26

A s jesus said in the Sermon on the Mount, animals live in the moment and get on with life. They teach us to avoid anxiety. They live simply. They can teach us. Remember that the Cynic philosophers emulated the dog's life. (Actually birds always look extremely anxious to me, with those paranoid head movements, but we get Christ's point.)

We love animals. And we love pets.

Why is this? It's because pets bring idling. They force us to switch off from the world of money and bosses and consuming. They make us take them on walks, during which we see trees and clouds and talk to neighbours. They bring us together with our families. It's such a joy to gaze at our pets. They inhabit a different world, a world of living in the moment, of complete freedom from guilt and anxiety. In the 19th century there was a craze for keeping birds as pets, in cages, and on perches. Parrots really were everywhere. Why? Because they're fascinating, non-industrial, unaffected by television news, joyful.

Now it's cats and dogs. Cats are idlers. They devote their lives to pleasure and sleep. They don't work, unless you count five minutes a day of hunting as work. At the same time, they do exactly what they want. They don't understand dogs. When we introduced our new puppy, Pilot, to our cat, Milly, who had been with us for over ten years, she looked at him, and then swiped his face with her paw. That set the tone for their relationship. Although she never hit him again, he left her alone and they lived together in something like harmony but also with complete mutual incomprehension.

The finest ponderer of cats was that most lovable of Renaissance writers, Montaigne, he who famously wrote, "When I play with my cat, how do I know that she is not playing with me rather than I with her?" Which itself is a statement of Montaigne's philosophical attitude: he does not declare; he wonders.

Dogs are not idlers, exactly. They love activity: sniffing, chasing, eating, barking, tail-wagging, being ridiculously cheerful. But they do like lying around doing nothing as well.

Our pets are our own domestic safari. They fill us with wonder because they live in a different world, with no worry for the morrow. They make us understand that objective reality does not exist: they see and inhabit a completely different world from ours. It looks different and it smells different.

Beyond pets, we love to study other animals through books or TV shows. In a recent issue of the *Idler* mag, we ran a great piece by a tortoise-breeder. He said that gazing at tortoises is enormously beneficial to good mental health. "If tortoises had a philosophy, it would be that – good or bad – 'this too shall pass' – which could be a steadying influence in these troubled times."

The *Idler*'s favourite animal, though, must be the sloth, and luckily we've had the great zoologist Lucy Cooke, founder of the Sloth Appreciation Society, writing for the magazine on this endearingly slow creature. Sloths are often ridiculed, but remember that Baloo the bear, in Kipling's *Jungle Book*, was a sloth bear, and he was the wisest animal in the jungle.

Cooke says that sloths are almost unbelievably chilled and non-violent, and won't even react much to loud noises. They are the Gandhis of the animal world:

It is believed by some that sloths' nerves have even evolved not to react to loud noises so they don't flinch and make themselves known if spooked. So there is no point saying boo to a sloth; he is simply too chilled out to notice.

This fact was discovered by the famous American naturalist William Beebe, who, back in the 1920s, when scientific endeavour was still a gentleman's sport, once spent ten days following a three-toed sloth around the rainforest.

"I have fired a gun close to a slumbering sloth, and to one feeding, and aroused but little attention," he states in his journal of the time.

They were probably hoping that if they ignored him, he'd leave them alone and aggravate something else in the name of science. But to no avail. Beebe kept up his sloth-bothering act for ten full days and nights during which time he poked and prodded and eventually managed to piss off one of the gentlest creatures on the planet.

At which point he noted: "When fully enraged, male sloths will, at this stage, slowly reach forward, open the mouth and attempt a languid bite."

Inaction points

☞ Get a dog or cat or tortoise.

☞ Consider the sloth.

☞ Watch the birds. Ornithology is a beautiful hobby for idlers.

8
Make a shed

I will arise and go now, and go to Innisfree,
And a small cabin build there, of clay and wattles made.
WB Yeats

VIRGINIA WOOLF SAID we need a room of our own to
retreat to and study in (she also said you need a private
income, but a shed is the more democratic option – most
people could build or buy a shed, but practically nobody
has a private income. Silly Virginia!)

For our purposes here, the word "shed" will have a pretty
wide meaning. It could include a room in the house where
you work, or a studio, or a man cave, or a corner of the
garage. It was amusing to me to read a piece in the *Financial
Times* recently about sheds. They chose a few to recommend to readers. But they didn't call them sheds. Mindful
of the aspirations of their go-getting readership, they called
these sheds "architect-designed garden workshop spaces".
And they were ridiculously expensive.

To buy or build a shed is one of the highest pleasures
known to man. At last you can become your own architect,
interior designer, artist, philosopher. When I visited the

39

comedian and artist Vic Reeves, I was delighted to discover that his garden has four sheds, one of which is his painting studio, to which he retreats each day at 8am and where he stays until 1pm.

A shed can be made on a very small budget. *Idler* contributor Graham Burnett made his for £500 and has inspired others to do the same thing. Wood can be got for free from old pallets (though you'll need a pallet-breaking tool and some time to break them up).

I don't have a shed in the literal sense. But I have a small office, about 20 minutes' bike ride from my home. It can fit four people, and sometimes it's full. But usually, it's just me on my own, or me and Victoria. To arrive here on my bicycle at 11am and stay until six, just working and pottering, and listening to music, feels like a great luxury. It's what even rich and successful people want. Damien Hirst, who can do whatever he wants, and always has done, travels each day from his house in west London to his studio by the river in Hammersmith and paints till six, then goes home. Damon Albarn likewise does a working day each day in his studio.

Yes, you can work at the kitchen table or in the library. But if you can find a room of your own or a shed or a studio, then happiness awaits. In sheds is peace. And with a shed you can be your own architect and designer.

George Bernard Shaw famously worked in a revolving shed. This was at a time, says Alex Johnson, the *Idler*'s sheds correspondent, when "there was growing appreciation of idyllic rural settings – a knock-on effect of which was that people had garden buildings installed. Shaw made the most of this movement, promoting himself as a reclusive thinker toiling in his rustic shelter, away from the intrusions of press and people alike, while at the same time inviting in newspapers and magazines and posing for photos."

Shaw's shed, says Johnson, was quite high tech:

Shaw's writing refuge was a six-square-metre wooden summerhouse, originally intended for his wife Charlotte and inspired by the similar set-up owned by his neighbour Apsley Cherry-Garrard, the naturalist who was part of Scott's expedition to the Antarctic, which he wrote up as *The Worst Journey in the World*. The hut was built on a revolving base that used castors on a circular track, essentially a shed on a lazy Susan. This meant the hut, at his home in Ayot St Lawrence, Hertfordshire, could be moved to improve the light or change the view (or indeed just for a bit of exercise). Spectacularly high tech for its time, it also had an electric heater and a telephone connection to the house as well as an alarm clock to alert the Nobel Prize winner that it was lunchtime. Shaw particularly enjoyed the isolation since it allowed the staff at the house with some degree of honesty to tell callers that "Mr Shaw is out" to prevent interruptions. He also called it "London" for the same reason ("I'm sorry Sir, Mr Shaw is in London").

In 1990, Shaw said to *World* magazine:

> Any place that will hold a bed and a writing table is as
> characteristic of me as any other.

Idlers should, though, in my view, avoid becoming total re-
cluses. After all, we are social beings. In an *Idler* magazine
published during the pandemic, we ran an extract from a
short story by Dickens about Mr Mopes the hermit. Mr
Mopes was based on the real-life hermit Mad Lucas, who
lived alone in squalour in a filthy cell on his dead parents'
country estate. Dickens hated him and was pretty clear
why: life was to be lived, not avoided. He describes the
hermit thus:

> A compound of Newgate, Bedlam, a debtors' prison in
> the worst time, a chimney sweep, a mudlark, and the
> Noble Savage!

After arguing with the unwashed Mr Mopes for a while,
Dickens gets to the nub of the matter: "We must arise and
wash our faces and do our gregarious work," he says, in
admonition of the filthy hermit's way of life.

On the other hand, let's not go as far as Dickens. He was
excessively active. He not only produced 15 of the greatest
novels ever written but also edited and published weekly
magazines, hurled himself into amateur dramatics, went
on 15-mile walks, toured the theatres with his one-man
show and ran a battered-wives' refuge. He probably worked

himself to death: he died at the age of 58 after a gruelling speaking tour of America.

So let us do our gregarious work, but also be good to that part of us that wants to go to Innisfree and build a cabin there of clay and wattles and live alone in a bee-loud glade. A shed is the answer.

Inaction points

☞ Go to idler.co.uk and search "shed".

☞ Draw your ideal shed on a piece of paper. Dreams start with a sketch.

9
Play ukulele

*There is nothing more notable in Socrates than that he
found time, when he was an old man, to learn music
and dancing, and thought it time well spent.*

Montaigne

UTTERLY POINTLESS AND totally uncool, we at the *Idler*
have long championed the ukulele as a friend to
happiness and the good life. (That's the ukulele that's
uncool and pointless, not we at the *Idler*.)

Like angling, playing the ukulele is sanctioned idling; it's
a way of doing nothing useful under the cover of learning
a musical instrument. It's the perfect skiving instrument.
Its' very pointlessness is its point: it provides us with an
escape from the jobs-money nexus. It is anti-utilitarian. It is
romantic. For me, it symbolises merriment.

And it's very portable. I have a few and keep one in the
office. Sometimes I find myself alone there, with a lot of
work to do. That is the perfect moment to pick up the uke,
practise "Pinball Wizard" and generally procrastinate for
an hour or so. You can keep a uke in the car and practise

when stuck in traffic or at the lights. Keep it by the bed or in the bathroom.

The uke can also help you to appreciate great music. Although it annoys my family immensely, I love to play the great baroque hits on my uke: Bach, Vivaldi, Pachelbel. I have a sort of cheat book which teaches you how to play simplified versions of *Spring*, *Winter* and *The Harmonious Blacksmith*. The act of learning these pieces helps you to get to know them better, and therefore intensifies your enjoyment when you're listening to the real thing.

When playing pop songs, you can sing at the same time, thus developing your singing voice. Again, this annoys my family as my singing is pretty atrocious. I tried to improve it by starting the Idler Choir, a weekly meeting of about 20 of us, under the guidance of choirmaster Tom Williams. I can just about sing if I lock on to the person next to me, but alone I still struggle to get the right notes. But I don't care.

When I talk about the ukulele with my philosopher friend Mark Vernon, he will talk of his love for the aeolian harp, which actually may have a greater claim to be the idler's instrument of choice, since it plays itself.

Here is a bit of Mark's philosophising on the subject:

I like the analogy of the philologist Owen Barfield: to be human is to be like an aeolian harp. These musical instruments consist of a wooden box and sounding board, over which strings are stretched across a bridge. They look a little like a violin without the neck. Also, they are not played by a bow, as the violin is, but rather by the wind. Aeolian harps are placed in openings across which the wind may blow, perhaps at a window: Aeolus is the god of the wind. As the air current sweeps across the strings, so the music from the harp is heard shifting and evolving, rising and falling. The analogy is that we are the harp, and the wind is the love required to make the music. We have a creative part to play in the harmonies that emerge, though without the movement of the pre-existing love there could be only silence.

Merry-making, said Robert Burton in his *Anatomy of Melancholy*, a very cheering book, eases depression, so alongside learning a musical instrument, we'd also suggest learning how to dance, or joining a choir.

If you really can't bear the ukulele, try the harmonica, nose flute, banjo or accordion. All great fun and portable and guaranteed to annoy everyone in your vicinity.

Inaction points

☞ Get yourself a ukulele. Spend at least fifty quid.

☞ Try the Idler Academy's ukulele course.

☞ Learn three chords: C, G and F. Now you have the basis of most pop music.

☞ Get yourself an aeolian harp.

☞ Find a dancing teacher. At festivals, we programme a brilliant ensemble called the Mudflappers. They get everyone doing swing moves to hip-hop in unison and it's pure joy.

10

Wander the city

For the perfect flâneur, for the passionate spectator,
it is an immense joy to set up house in the heart of the
multitude, amid the ebb and flow of movement,
in the midst of the fugitive and the infinite.
Baudelaire

WHEN I WAS A COUNTRY MOUSE, I would receive letters from readers saying something like, "It's all very well for you, being idle in the countryside. I live in the busy city. What am I supposed to do?"

But of course the city offers plentiful opportunities for idling, if you look. The literary critic Walter Benjamin famously resurrected the 18th-century notion of the *flâneur*, the drifting poet, wandering through Paris. It's an idea that modern psychogeographers cleave to: there is poetry and romance and wonder in the heart of the commercial tumult. There is beauty in the busy world, in the arcades, in the clothes of the people, in the electric lights.

And it's not only the Parisians who can claim to be idlers in the city. I was recently alerted to the Bulgarian custom of *aylyak* by my correspondent Bernard Marszalek of Berkeley,

California. He says that *aylyak* is a tradition associated with the Bulgarian city of Plovdiv. The word is derived from a Turkish word meaning "idleness" but its meaning today is a little closer to "unhurried conviviality". *Aylyak* is all about hanging out in the city.

While wandering round Plovdiv, a BBC reporter asked Bulgarian actor, director and mime artist Plamen Radev Georgiev to define the concept.

"It was tied in with social status," said the report, "with a kind of dandyish wandering the streets with nothing to do. And, on a deeper level – Georgiev called this 'Zen *aylyak*' – it was to do with freedom of the soul. '*Aylyak* means that you can be engaged with the difficulties of life, but you remain safe from all life's problems,' Georgiev said."

The BBC reporter also quotes this charming 1906 description of an evening in Plovdiv – then called Philippopolis – by travel writer John Foster Fraser:

> Picture the scene. A garden, lit with many lamps. Beneath the trees innumerable tables. At the tables sat "all Philippopolis" sipping coffee, drinking beer, toasting one another in litres of wine. At one end of the garden was a little stage. There was a Hungarian band which played rhapsodically…It was Sunday night and Philippopolis was enjoying itself.

I'm not sure what the British equivalent would be. Perhaps we could call it the art of sitting around doing nothing in particular – or *sitten*.

During lockdown, in common with millions of others, I developed a new appreciation of the world on my doorstep. Victoria and I wandered down the Thames. I took a day off and walked with a few mates about 15 miles along the canals of London town, from west to east London. We talked, drifted and saw both herons and smoking chimneys. Industry and wild flowers lived together. Elderflowers grew from the cracks in the pavement.

Nature is a misnomer: fields are, after all, man-made, and nature and beauty can be found in the city. The view from Westminster Bridge in the morning, said Wordsworth, is just as calming as the great outdoors – and he should know, he's the nature poet:

Never did sun more beautifully steep
In his first splendour, valley, rock, or hill;
Ne'er saw I, never felt, a calm so deep!

So if you can see and feel an unusually deep calm by just standing on a bridge, then why make the effort to leave the city in search of inner peace?

Inaction points
☞ Stroll about, take your time.
☞ Read Baudelaire.
☞ Find a bridge. Lean over the side.

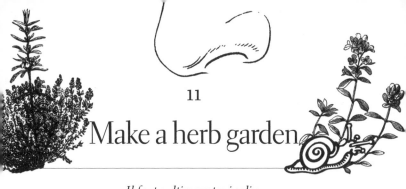

11

Make a herb garden

Il faut cultiver votre jardin.
Voltaire

CULTIVATING PLANTS is satisfying, is therapeutic and opens up idle time in your life.

I'd hesitate, however, before recommending taking on a whole allotment. They're an enormous amount of work. For many years, while living in a dilapidated Devon farmhouse, I maintained, or attempted to maintain, a vegetable patch which was around half the size of an allotment. I had plenty of time in my life, as I worked four hours a day on my writing, and had the rest of the day free. I managed to get some good food out of it, while spending many enjoyable hours digging and planting. Yes, it was fun to dig up carrots and potatoes and tend cabbages. But the savings on buying them from the shop were negligible. I found it difficult to give the patch the time it really needed, and it got overgrown. Eventually I gave up. Now we live in London and we have five Syrian and Lebanese supermarkets within five minutes of the front door. And we get vegetables delivered by Riverford Organic, a home delivery box system.

So I don't bother with vegetable-growing any more. It's fun to buy them. Just try to buy them locally, and make friends with the shopkeepers. Then shopping itself can become an idle pleasure, convivial, fun, rather than a solitary burden.

Victoria and I do, however, keep a few pots of herbs.

The advice offered by the laudable permaculture movement is to grow stuff that you use regularly, and to keep the pots or beds near the kitchen door. An allotment is too far away from your house. So now we have rosemary, mint, parsley and oregano in the front garden. They're all terribly easy to grow, and probably best kept in pots rather than grown in beds, simply because in beds they tend to grow too well and to take over. In a pot, you can keep the herb contained. We've tried growing basil and have had no luck, so conclude it's best to buy it.

Herbs are constantly useful and we've lately discovered that if you have a steady supply, there is absolutely no need to waste money on expensive pre-prepared herbal teas. Just chuck a bit of rosemary and oregano in very hot water and steep for five minutes. Mint likewise.

Tending a few plants, looking after them, watching them grow buds, and fruit, and then die back, is one of the great wonders of the world. And in creating your own modest herb garden, you'll be bringing yet another monklike pleasure into your life.

Inaction points

☞ Buy four pots, four plants and a bag of compost.

☞ Rosemary, parsley, mint, oregano and nasturtiums are very easy to grow.

☞ Basil is tricky. Don't bother.

☞ Keep your pots of herbs very near the kitchen.

12

Get out into the woods (or parks)

This was my prayer: a piece of land, not of great size,
With a garden, and a permanent spring near the house,
And above them a stretch of woodland.
Ovid

WE AT THE *IDLER* wouldn't be the first to recommend the healing pleasures of being in nature and we won't be the last. The Taoist philosophers of ancient China banged on about the therapeutic benefits of rivers and mountains and woods. Wordsworth and Coleridge conceived their poetic revolution while wandering the Quantocks in the west of England. Horace loved the great outdoors.

You don't need to go far for a wood. You don't have to own one. Instead, go to the shared woods, the trees in the park, the nature reserves. City parks improve all the time. Berlin is covered in semi-wild vegetable gardens with hipster cafés; London's parks get better every year with long grass and meadow areas now in vogue. Hyde Park in

London has plenty of trees, and go just a little further to Richmond for the delights of its walled park, first built for Henry VIII, but now open to all, and full of lovely old gnarled trees.

Petrarch, writing in the early-14th century, was very clear about who led the better life, idler or banker. In this lovely passage, from a book called *The Life of Solitude*, he compares the life of a banker in the medieval city with the life of a woodland-dwelling recluse, a country mouse:

> The busy man, a hapless dweller of the city, awakes in the middle of the night, his sleep interrupted by his cares or the cries of his clients, often even by fear of the light and by terror of nightly visions. No sooner is he up than he settles his body to the miserable bench and applies his mind to falsehood. On treachery his heart is wholly fixed – whether he meditates driving a corrupt bargain, betraying his friend or his ward, assailing with his seductions his neighbour's wife whose only refuge is her chastity, spreading the veil of justice over a litigious quarrel, or whatever other mischief of a public or private character he intends. Now eager with passion and aflame with desire, and now frozen with desperation, like a very bad workman, he begins before dawn the web of the daily toil in which he shall involve others with himself.
>
> The retired man – the man of leisure – awakes in a happy mood, refreshed by moderate rest and a short sleep, unbroken unless he is aroused at intervals by the

songs of night-haunting Philomel. When he has shaken himself lightly from his couch and, banishing thoughts of his body, begun to intone in the calm hours, he summons the Lord to strengthen his heart. No pleasures of the busy man, no luxury of city life, no pomp of kingdoms can match his state. Looking up from his place to the starry heaven [...] he turns immediately to the study of some honest and agreeable lesson, and so nourished with the most delightful food, he awaits the coming of light with great composure of mind.

The longed-for light has now arrived to their differing prayers, and the busy man's doorway is beset by enemies and friends. He is greeted, solicited, pulled in one direction, jostled in another, assailed with arguments, and rent asunder. The retired man finds a free doorway, and he has the choice of remaining where he is or going whithersoever his mind disposes him.

The busy man, loaded with complaints and affairs, goes in troubled spirits to the courts, and the beginning of his cruel day is marked by lawsuits. The retired man, with store of leisure and of calm, goes blithely into a nearby wood and enters joyfully upon the propitious threshold of a serene day.

You don't need to be a full-time country mouse, though. The banker can find respite from his cares in nearby woods. In lockdown, Victoria and I discovered that we could drive for 45 minutes from west London and find ourselves in the most beautiful woods. In the winter we walked on frozen mud among skeletal trees. In spring we foraged for wild garlic or *allium ursinum*, which is absolutely delicious, and very easy to identify. We walked through fields of sheep and down ancient tracks.

Do you really want an Epicurean villa? I would counsel against the immense cost and work involved in buying a second home. It is lovely to dream about, as Horace did, but my view is that you're better off with one home. Then you'll be free to do whatever you want at weekends and holidays. Stay with others. I write this from Tuscany where I'm staying with a friend. If I had a hut or cottage in a wood somewhere, I might have decided to stay there.

From the city you can cycle out, get the train, drive down the motorway. It does not take long to get into the woods.

Inaction points
☞ Find woods near where you live.
☞ Do not covet a second home.

13

Chuck the smartphone

IF YOU'D LIKE to introduce some more idle time into your life, learn to think again, and save a fortune in the process, then why not get rid of your smartphone and replace it with a dumb phone, or at least a phone of average intelligence?

Do you really need a smartphone? I personally ditched mine many years ago. In many ways this has been blissful. Whole swathes of idling time are opened up to me. On the train I stare out of the window and meditate. If the bus is late I relish the opportunity to sit and do nothing. I am not targeted by ads. Since I don't have a Facebook or a Twitter account either, I can wander round like a sort of digital ascetic, feeling superior, gazing at the flowers and not taking photographs of everything I see and putting them on Instagram. On walks I am undisturbed. If the Epicureans were right, and the goal of life is undisturbedness, then ditching the smartphone would seem to be an obvious strategy.

My problem is that not more people have done as I have done. I seem to be literally the only person in the world without a smartphone. Even the best-selling Buddhist monk Haemin Sunim was glued to his smartphone when he gave a talk at an *Idler* dinner recently.

This makes me feel left out and lonely. People send me pictures and links which I cannot see. I am excluded from WhatsApp chats. I cannot show friends amusing pictures on my phone. I cannot take selfies or quick snaps.

I wander lonely, excluded from the cloud.

But actually, I don't care. The pros of freedom outweigh the cons of not seeing a friend's Instagram snaps of their holiday (by quite a long way).

I had one friend, D, who didn't have a smartphone. Then I bumped into him the other day and he got out an iPhone. "Judas!", I cried. "Sorry," he said, and shrugged.

I can't work out whether I am being deliberately perverse or whether I have made a sensible choice which is good for my mental health. And as I say, if it is such a good idea, why don't more people do it? It saves money and makes you happy. It's surely a no-brainer.

My friend and fellow smartphone-rejector James Parker recently wrote a great piece for *The Atlantic* where he mused on his love for his flip phone. He puts it so well:

You are not connected to the internet. So for me, you are a little ebony brick of privacy. And by *privacy* I don't mean cookies or my Social Security number or whatever – I mean the fragile sphere of imagination in which I exist when I'm not diddling about online. I mean what's left of my non-digital self. When I clack your two halves shut, you glorious techno-mollusk, that's it. Sauron cannot see me.

Second, you've become rather talismanic, socially. You stand for something. Perversity? Willed obsolescence? Sure, why not. It's like hanging around with a maladaptive friend: I enjoy watching people react to you. When I brandish you, flourish you, wield you in the world, I get exclamations of pity and confusion.

Strangely, or not strangely, James and I were in a band together at university, a punk band, and I recently met up with another member whom I hadn't seen for 20 years, and, rather brilliantly, he also had a dumbphone.

Punk rock till I die.

I do, I confess, keep a mini iPad so I do not feel completely disconnected from so-called reality. My own phone is called a Punkt, and it can be used as a hotspot. So if very necessary I can sit down with my iPad and phone and do some emailing.

Another tip is to switch your phone's screen to black and white, which I believe you can do by pressing one of its buttons three times. The black-and-white screen is less aggressive and demanding than the colour screen. I imagine that the colours of the buttons on your phone have been selected by eminent psychologists in the field of colour theory, behavioural scientists who know what makes you click. A black-and-white screen will clearly disable their fiendish plans.

Inaction points

☞ Give your smartphone to a teenager.
☞ Find dumbphone articles at Idler website.
☞ Buy one. Acres of idle time will open up for you.

14
Be near water

The supreme good is like water,
which nourishes all things without trying to.
It is content with the low places that people disdain.
Thus it is like the Tao.

Lao Tzu

W HEN LARKING ABOUT in the *Idler* office, we like to
spot examples of silly neologisms or what we call
"formerly known as". One good example of this phenome-
non is "wild swimming", formerly known as swimming.
Over the last ten years or so the simple act of swimming
now has the word "wild" appended to it in order to make it
sound like something new when in fact of course swimming in lakes and rivers is as old as the lakes and rivers
themselves.

Under lockdowns, swimming in the sea and in rivers
enjoyed a renaissance. This is good for me. I never liked
swimming pools, with their stink of chlorine, competitive
atmosphere, vanity, weird shouty acoustics and verrucas.
Absolutely horrific.

Far better to be near a river or the sea. Living in London,

we used lockdowns to explore the Thames, walking along it, cycling along it, staring at it, kayaking in it, swimming in it. One evening we got in a little motor boat owned by our friends Mr and Mrs Steerstrait. Mr Steerstrait works in marine insurance and has an interest in boats. We ate fine breads and cheeses and drank fancy beers as we pootled along from Chiswick to Richmond. It was bliss.

Another time Victoria and I discovered a secluded spot on the Thames near Oxford, not far from where Lewis Carroll rowed with Dean Liddell's daughters Alice, Edina and Lorina, and we swam there at weekends.

Why does water attract us? Again, I think it's because it offers us a world free of striving and goal-centred activity. Like diary-writing, it offers a bit of respite from worldly cares and the industrial complex. It's slow, too.

And all the world over human beings appear to love being on the beach or being on a river or even floating down a grotty canal. I'm quite jealous of people who live in Brighton; they have the sea as a constant presence.

When we are free, Victoria and I, like thousands of others, like to go and camp near a beach. We love the Pembrokeshire coast in Wales, and have spent happy days living in a caravan on a campsite. Rich and busy people seek to cut themselves off from the vulgar hordes, but we ordinary folk love piling onto beaches and being together near water, splashing, standing still and being in the moment. It's amazing, on a beach, to look at how many people are simply standing or sitting and staring at the sea, doing nothing – not talking, not reading. At the seaside or by the river, doing nothing is encouraged. Hence the appeal.

Being on the beach can be like a mini-festival. Everyone has come together to celebrate a common interest. The normal rules do not apply.

Inaction points

☞ Find a river or beach.
☞ Bathe. Stare. Stand still.

15

Sit on a public bench

On the way back from the shop, sit on a bench, shut your
eyes for five minutes and listen to whatever sounds are
in the air, be they cars, birds, aeroplanes or sirens.
Be silent. That's the meditation done.
Arthur Smith

THERE ARE FREE AIDS to idling dotted about in most
cities, and they don't get enough press, in my view.

They are the public benches. I wonder who invented
them. They are probably an ancient idea, and an extremely
good one.

The bench is always there for you. Earlier I talked about
forms of meditation and I mentioned bench yoga as invented by the comedian and Epicurean philosopher Arthur
Smith. In his recent memoir, he gave the above top tip for
happiness.

Arthur Smith also told me that he loves those inscrip-
tions you see on benches, the *in memoriam* ones: "Sid used
to love to sit here." It would be nice to have a bench
inscribed with your name after your death. "Tom used to
love idling on this spot."

I once put quite a lot of effort into an "art bench" scheme. My idea was that the council would commission artists to create a bench. So you could sit on art. I talked to some people at Islington Council but they put me off by saying that benches were more complicated than they looked. They needed to pass certain health and safety standards. I eventually gave up.

I did send my "art bench" proposal to the Bristol City of Ideas competition, and started to get quite excited, as I was certain that the idea would be far superior to any other idea submitted, and that the councillors in Bristol would be more progressive and art-friendly than the ones in Islington. Needless to say, I never got a reply.

Benches were a saviour during lockdowns. They were used as meeting places, lunch venues, pubs, libraries, meditation zones and nap spots. And many of us are going to continue to make use of this marvellous public resource. Truly, the authorities are not all bad.

Inaction point

☞ Find a bench, preferably a wooden one, and sit on it. Do nothing.

16

Seek an altered state

*I took my [mescaline] pill at eleven … I spent several
minutes – or was it several centuries? – not merely gazing
at those bamboo legs, but actually being them – or rather
being myself in them; or, to be still more accurate
(for "I" was not involved in the case, nor in a
certain sense were "they") being my Not-self
in the Not-self which was the chair.*

Aldous Huxley

I'VE TAKEN MY FAIR share of drugs. I started in my teens
with tobacco and beer, and soon graduated to hash.
At university, inspired by a weird offshoot of American
punk called Straight Edge, I became briefly sober. In my
twenties I discovered ecstasy and raving, and then in my
later twenties cocktails, cocaine and members' clubs. I did
attempt to keep taking ecstasy occasionally after having
children, but the results were fairly disastrous.

However, I am very open to resuming drug-taking in my
fifties but in the spirit of self-experimentation, not hedon-
ism, like Aldous Huxley and his doors of perception. And it
seems I am not alone. There are lots of middle-aged men

and women out there who are talking about magic mushrooms again. Psychedelics are getting respectable.

Till recently, psychedelics were illegal. Journalist Michael Pollan, in his book *This Is Your Mind on Plants*, asks why the psychoactive drug caffeine is accepted and promoted the world over yet opium and psychedelics are frowned upon. The answer is because the altered states induced by the latter two could make you question the work ethic and capitalism in general and wonder, what's the point? Whereas the former, which after all fuelled London's growth as a centre of finance in the 17th and 18th centuries, is a handmaiden to hard work and helps you to slave more efficiently for the mill owner. McDonald's sells it for £1.

At the forefront of new work on the therapeutic value of psychedelics is Dr Robin Carhart-Harris, who began his research at Imperial College in London and now works in California. I interviewed him at the Idler Festival in July 2018.

TOM HODGKINSON: How did you get into this line of work, Robin?

ROBIN CARHART-HARRIS: Academically, psychology led me into it, the idea that the mind runs deeper than we ordinarily think. There exists a class of drugs, psychedelics, that can unfurl the mind and reveal its contents. They're called "mind revealing" – that's what psychedelic means. It just opened up a world of fascination for me, which has never let up.

TH: I was growing up, this stuff wasn't around but it was legendary because I was reading Aldous Huxley's *The Doors of Perception*. We were finding out about acid-taking in the '60s.

RCH: "Turn on, tune in, drop out!", as Timothy Leary said. There was a feeling among the establishment that psychedelics fuelled counter-cultural thinking, anarchic thinking, and that was frightening.

TH: I was fascinated. I read about Ken Kesey, the Merry Pranksters, the Tom Wolfe books and then something happened, it just vanished. During the '50s, according to Michael Pollan's excellent new book *How to Change Your Mind*, psychedelic research seemed to be quite respectable. What happened?

RCH: That's absolutely true. It was very much part of the mainstream: Cary Grant had extensive LSD psychotherapy, Robert Kennedy's wife had LSD psychotherapy and he actually argued against the legislation that came in towards the end of the '60s. Later on, it transpired that LSD was seen as a threat, a societal threat, a psychological threat. There was a feeling among the establishment that psychedelics fuelled counter-cultural thinking, anarchic thinking, and that was frightening. There are clear examples of people within the Nixon administration essentially admitting that this is why they legislated against it. They were frightened of LSD and they were frightened of Timothy Leary telling people to experiment.

TH: Do you think Timothy Leary was partly to blame for

holding back the progress of psychedelic research because there was something a bit chauvinistic about him, almost like a false guru character?

RCH: In a way, what happened with Leary reflects what happened more generally. He started out as a mainstream figure: he was a psychology professor at Harvard, he conducted credible research and he actually coined two of the most important terms in psychedelic research and psychedelic therapy, "set" and "setting". Then he went off the rails, maybe through taking too much of the stuff, and became a self-proclaimed high priest of LSD. He started being quite irresponsible with his messages, and also the substance to his preaching was pretty loose. And so, he fell out of favour with the mainstream who wanted him to stick to the integrity of science.

TH: And so the whole thing was derailed pretty much in 1971, right?

RCH: In '71, the United Nations Misuse of Drugs Act was passed, which carried over to the UK. We fell in line with the US on drugs despite evidence that on balance – and my boss at Imperial, David Nutt, is known for promoting this view — psychedelics aren't one of the more dangerous categories of drugs. They're being classified as Class A drugs and according to those criteria, they have no recognisable medicinal value. The science just doesn't fit that.

TH: In one of your studies, you carried out a trial with 20 people for whom the conventional treatments for depression didn't work. Can you describe what they might have been through before they came to your trial?

RCH: They'd tried all different types of antidepressants. Some had tried as many as 11 different varieties. Virtually all of them had tried psychotherapy, often a few different varieties. Some had even tried electro-convulsive therapy. They'd thrown the kitchen sink at their depression and nothing had worked, so we thought we'd try magic mushrooms. We'd done some brain-imagery work in London that supported the idea that magic mushrooms could have antidepres-sant properties and so we gave it a whirl. They were in a clinical-research facility but we massively trans-formed it — we had drapes and low lighting.

TH: So you made it look like a chill-out room at a rave?

RCH: Yeah, sort of. The music wasn't far off either.

TH: Sven Väth and Aphex Twin playing?

RCH: Yes, and some Brian Eno. People lay there with their eyes closed.

TH: The magic mushrooms you use are called liberty cap, an indigenous hallucinogen of the UK. The doses were somewhat higher than I was expecting – would they typically get about 40 magic mushrooms?

RCH: Apparently they grow on Hampstead Heath! Typically people would need to take around ten to feel the effects; we're giving something more like 50. That's intentional: we're trying to induce a transformative experience. When someone has been thoroughly depressed all of their adult life, then you want a trans-formation. People describe their experiences using terms like "mystical", "spiritual" — they describe their normal sense of self dissolving.

TH: How long would this 50-magic-mushroom trip last for?

RCH: About four or five hours, with a strong peak about an hour and a half in.

TH: And what was the conclusion of the study?

RCH: Well, it seemed to work! Everyone's depression score dropped. But that can happen with any kind of inter-vention – it happens with placebo. So you can look at the magnitude of the drop and then how sustained it is. Going on three months, six months, 12 months, we're still seeing significant drops. That said, people do relapse and sometimes they go back onto other medications and other treatments after around six months. But to have that window of relief and to know that it's possible they describe as so, so valuable.

So let us study the psychedelics. Even a modest dose of magic mushrooms can help you to see the world a little differently, to get a bit of distance from your quotidian real-ity, and to dissolve anxiety. Essentially, they reduce the ego (though living with Victoria, I can tell you, my ego doesn't require any more dissolving, ha ha).

Inaction points

☞ On no account take any mind-bending drug or illegal substance!

☞ Read books by Michael Pollan. He's written the best books about drugs of contemporary times.

☞ Take Robin Carhart-Harris's Idler Academy course.

17

Take a tea break
(and a lunch break and a coffee break)

*There are few hours in life more agreeable than the hour
dedicated to the ceremony known as afternoon tea.*
Henry James

YOU KNOW THAT the secret to bringing more idling into
your life is to schedule it? That idea came up in
Chapter 2 in a discussion about discussing Michael Palin's
diary habit. Somehow it helps to have an outside authority
telling you to be idle, even if that outside authority is
actually you.

Under lockdown, many people enjoyed being idle
because they were told to be idle by their governments. It
was the only time in living memory when governments,
which are generally fierce adherents to the work ethic,
were telling us to stay in bed and avoid work – extraordinary
really.

The effect of being told to be idle, for many, is that the
guilt associated with being idle was completely removed.
It's my patriotic duty to be idle, it's not an indulgence!

So let's help ourselves by telling ourselves to be idle more often. Thanks to the untiring work of the unions, the working day used to have little punctuation moments built into it. Tea breaks, lunch hour, coffee breaks. These have largely disappeared, ripped from us by our boring utilitarian leaders. But as Lin Yutang, the great Chinese-American writer, put it, "There is something in the nature of tea that leads us into a world of quiet contemplation of life." Tea brings idling.

So you must do it. Don't wait for someone else to give it to you. Take your time. Take back your time. Give yourself two hours of idle time every day, meaning at least an hour for lunch and half an hour for tea, and half an hour for elevenses as well. These delicious gaps in the day will feed your mind and once again provide a break from dreary utilitarian life.

When taking tea at 4 o'clock, or elevenses, don't slurp your mug at the desk. Make an effort to take it outdoors. Pick up a chair and place it elsewhere. Take pride in doing literally nothing during your tea break. Don't just do something, sit there.

Inaction points
☞ Make a pot of tea at 4pm and savour it, like a Chinese tea ritual.
☞ Take it with cake.
☞ Try different locations for your tea and other breaks.
☞ Schedule your breaks in your calendar.

18

Lie down

Nature does not hurry,
yet everything is accomplished.
Lao Tzu

MY FAVOURITE OF THE many great songs by the late
Neil Innes must be "Lie Down and Be Counted".

Just to remind you, the chorus of this stirring idler's
anthem encourages us to stop standing for all the terrible
things life throws at us, and to lie down as an act of resistance. It's a Gandhiesque message.

Noble and visionary sentiments indeed and I was re-
minded of the song lately when reading a news story about
a new wave of rebellious Chinese youth who are apparently
obeying Innes's injunction.

The new movement is called Lying Flat or Tang Ping,
and its followers advocate lying down rather than joining
the rat race which, as the Specials' Terry Hall correctly
pointed out, is a waste of your time.

Tang Ping is inspired by the example of Cynic philosopher Diogenes, who, as we heard earlier, threw away all his

possessions and lived like a dog in an upturned wine cask in Athens.

Now nihilistic millennials have surveyed what the authorities have got mapped out and have concluded, like Jarvis Cocker, that it's nothing much to shout about.

Tang Ping appears to have its origins in a blog post by young Luo Huazhong, a former factory worker who quit his job, reduced his outgoings and got by on odd jobs.

"I have been chilling," Mr Luo, 31, wrote. "I don't feel like there's anything wrong."

China's new work ethic has had the effect of completely knackering and depressing its people. It has been nick-named 9-9-6. That means working from nine till nine, six days a week. If my calculations are correct, that makes 72 hours. INSANITY. Even the notoriously tough workhouses in England in the 19th century demanded only a 50 hour week, and the inmates were encouraged to sleep ten hours a night.

Tang Ping gathered 200,000 followers on social media, but the authorities then censored Tang Ping-related posts and the newspapers have called the movement "shameful". Even the hard-working utilitarian corporate capitalists at the *Economist* magazine have taken notice and ran a report with the headline "China urges its people to struggle. Some say no."

Tang Ping reminds me very much of the English punk movement in the 1970s. Johnny Rotten sang various anti-work lyrics including "I don't work, I just feed, that's all I need" and "I'm a lazy sod", and both The Clash and The Specials raged against crap jobs and "the system", singing "I won't open a letter bomb for you" and "You'll be working for the rat race".

The Chinese millennials are in fact the new Taoists. The country has always battled between the Confucian ideals of harmony and social conformity and the hippy ideals of Lao Tzu, founder of Taoism, who hymned the joys of sitting quietly by a river writing poetry rather than kowtowing at the court.

Mr Luo has defended himself by arguing that his actions, or lack of them, hurt no one.

"Those people who say lying down is shameful are shameless," he said. "I have the right to choose a slow life-style. I didn't do anything destructive to society. Do we have to work 12 hours a day in a sweatshop, and is that justice?"

Another Tang Ping advocate is Zhang Xinmin, who quit his job in advertising to concentrate on his music. He wrote a distinctly Taoist song called "Tang Ping Is the Right Way". It was promptly removed by the authorities. "Nowadays," he complained, "only running forward is allowed, but not lying down." His song includes lyrics such as "Lying down saves energy, and saves the planet" and "Lying down is the royal way". The less censorious platform YouTube has not banned the song, however, and you can see it there, along with a clutch of approving comments from American millennials.

Inaction point

☞ Find a sofa, bed or hammock and lie on it.

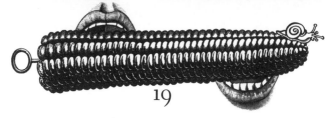

19

Throw a feast

O heavenly night-time dinners, when I and my friends
Eat beside my own Lar, and feed jostling servants
On left-over offerings. Each guest drinks as he wishes
Large glasses or small, free from foolish rules, whether
He downs the strong stuff, nobly, or wets his whistle
In more carefree style. And so the conversation starts.

Horace

[A Lar was a spirit that protected the household]

Back in the 1930s G K Chesterton teased his readers for getting Christmas wrong. "The Christmas season is domestic," he wrote, "and for that reason most people now prepare for it by struggling in tramcars, standing in queues, rushing away in trains, crowding despairingly into tea-shops, and wondering whether they will ever get home."

Far better, he argued, that we stay at home and simply muck about, and play games: "If Christmas could become more domestic, instead of less, I believe there could be a vast increase in the real Christmas spirit; the spirit of the Child." I think this is true of feasts in general, and though most of us might recoil at the cruelty of Horace and his mates, feeding left-overs to crowds of jostling servants, the other details of his fantasy feast ring true. It's about freedom, food and conversation.

What is Christmas really all about? What is a feast for? Let us go back to the 14th century, when the idea of a merry Christmas was taking hold. The medieval Christmas was all about feasting and dancing, and this is the sort of Christmas that was celebrated at Camelot, according to the great medieval poem *Sir Gawain and the Green Knight*. Christmas in those days really did last 12 days or longer, and that was 12 days when the shops closed and no one was allowed to work. Instead, you should play games and eat and generally have fun:

> For there the feast was alike full fifteen days,
> with all the meat and mirth men could devise:
> such clamour and glee glorious to hear
> dear din in the daylight, dancing of nights;
> all was happiness high in halls and chambers
> with lords and ladies.

Bloody brilliant! Fifteen days off for Christmas.

Of course, Christmas wasn't invented in medieval times. Throwing a midwinter feast, lighting the fire, lighting candles and decorating the inside of the house with evergreens are all fairly obvious ways of cheering oneself up when it is cold outside. They are customs that have persisted for perhaps thousands of years, and withstood the full frontal attack on Christmas which came later.

We know from very early Christians that Christmas was celebrated on 25 December, as that was the traditional date for the birth of the sun. In the 4th century, the Scriptor Cyrus wrote:

It was a custom of the pagans to celebrate on the same 25 December the birthday of the Sun, at which they kindled lights in token of festivity. In these solemnities and rituals the Christians also took part. Accordingly when the doctors of the Church perceived that the Christians had a leaning to this festival, they took counsel and resolved that the true nativity should be solemnised on that day.

Christmas is also related to the Roman feast of Saturnalia. This began on 17 December and lasted up to seven days. Shops, schools and lawcourts were closed; there was general noisy rejoicing. Candles were exchanged. A mock king could be appointed. The writer Lucian said that one person would be voted sole king of all "so that you not only escape silly orders but can give them yourself, telling one man to shout out something disgraceful about himself, another to dance naked, pick up the flute girl and carry her three times around the room."

Invaders adapted the feast. In the 11th century the Danes ruled England and introduced the word "Yule" – the Scandinavian term for Christmas. Now they are influencing us again with their *hygge* export – the philosophy of cosiness and lighting candles.

Holly and ivy were the natural choices of decoration because they grew wild right outside the house. A 15th-century poem proclaimed:

> *Nay, ivy, nay, it shall not be, I wys,*
> *holly have the master as the manner is,*
> *Holly stood in the hall, fair to behold,*
> *Ivy stood without the door, she is full sore-a-cold.*

Account books of the late-medieval and early-Tudor period show that candles were ordered in huge quantities by churches and cathedrals. Candles brought light in the darkness.

You were encouraged to be hospitable at Christmas, and open your doors to the less fortunate. The Tudor writer Thomas Tusser said:

> At Christmas we banquet, the rich with the poor,
> Who then (but the miser?) but openeth his door?

Many aristos did in fact open their doors. According to historian Ronald Hutton, the Earl of Northumberland had four swans for dinner and received large numbers of clerical dignitaries. The Mayor of Coventry kept "open house" for all. The Duke of Buckingham employed a troupe of French players, three jesters, the municipal musicians of Bristol and an acrobat. Plus there was card-playing and board-gaming, as today.

One year, Hutton records, Richard II had 20,000 guests who consumed 200 oxen and 200 tubs of wine.

A Christmas dinner provided by Henry V offered brawn, dates with mottled cream, carp, prawns, turbot, tench, perch, fresh sturgeon with whelks, roasted porpoise, crayfish, roasted eels and lampreys, leached meats garnished with hawthorn leaves, and marzipan.

Christmas, like Saturnalia, has always been the season for a certain amount of legitimised disorder. Each year a Lord of Misrule was appointed and given throne, canopy, armoury, jester and a gibbet for hanging those who displeased him. An echo of this is seen today in the drunks wearing antler horns and swaying around the streets at night. That is the true spirit of Christmas: anarchy.

So let us throw frequent feasts throughout the year. There are plenty of excuses: birthdays, saints' days, anniversaries, celebrations. You don't need me to tell you when to throw a feast. But throw a feast you must. Just skip the bit about feeding left-overs to jostling servants.

Inaction points

☞ Ask guests to bring a dish.

☞ Drink wine.

☞ Light candles.

☞ Strew greenery everywhere.

☞ Get some musicians to play.

20

Play old games

*I love everything that's old: old friends, old times,
old manners, old books, old wine.*
Mr Hardcastle in *She Stoops to Conquer*
by Oliver Goldsmith

TO THE ABOVE LIST, enumerated with such charm and
style, I would certainly add "old games".

New games – by which I mean computer games like
Call of Duty: Black Ops and *Grand Theft Auto* are anti-idle.
They promote aggressive capitalist values like greed and
violence and driving cars at high speeds. (My teenage son
may well not agree with me on this issue.) Another horrific
computer game I encountered – in fact a piece of work
ethic propaganda – is a game called *Job Island: Hard
Working People*, about which the less said the better.

The old games, being old, have no brainwashing inten-
tion. They do not feed the system. They are merely for fun.
Like most of the ideas in this book, games remove us from
the world of jobs and money and place us in another world,
where pointless fun is the order of the day.

At the top of the hierarchy of the old games is chess, but to the list of tried and tested pastimes, let me add the following:

Draughts
Be warned, you may get seriously addicted. Draughts is a far more complex game than it appears.

Backgammon
Again, backgammon is endlessly satisfying. Add the doubling dice and you introduce a thrilling gambling element.

Nine Men's Morris
To be played by any age. The sort of game that can surprise you: just when you think you are winning, your opponent pulls an amazing move out of the hat.

Any card game
A better game than a pack of cards has never been invented. For a few quid, you have in your pocket an almost infinite variety of games.

Tennis
Apart from cycling, tennis is the only physical exercise I take, and I love every moment. All problems disappear with the exception of getting the ball over the net and into the opponent's court. As you know, it's a Victorian invention but is based on real tennis which itself has its roots in the streets of Italian city states.

Croquet

The finest game of all. If you can find a real croquet lawn, you are in heaven, but a smaller one will do. The writer Craig Brown spends the morning writing and the afternoon playing croquet. It's the ideal life.

Noughts and Crosses

Beautifully simple. All that's needed is a piece of paper and a pencil.

Scissors, Paper, Stone

This is the game that needs nothing at all.

Hangman

Fun and educational too.

Inaction points

☞ Consider creating a games cupboard containing chess, backgammon, cards and so on.

☞ Join a croquet club.

☞ Set aside an hour of games time each day.

☞ Avoid stressful, violent dramas on the television.

21

Take a day off

The question isn't, "What are we going to do?"
The question is, "What aren't we going to do?"
Ferris Bueller

MOST OF US are aware of that excellent movie *Ferris Bueller's Day Off*, which follows a group of well-to-do skiving high-school students. It's a witty celebration of ingenuity and resistance to authority and a must-see for all idlers. A list of great idler-friendly films would probably also include Charlie Chaplin's *Modern Times*, *Quadrophenia* and *Brazil*, all of which deal with squashing of the spirit by industrial society.

Fewer are aware of the poem "William Wordsworth's Day Off". OK, that's not its real name. It's actually called *Lines Written for His Sister* and featured in Wordsworth and Coleridge's breakthrough collection, *Lyrical Ballads*, first published in 1798.

Here are the first four stanzas:

It is the first mild day of March:
Each minute sweeter than before
The redbreast sings from the tall larch
That stands beside our door.

There is a blessing in the air
Which seems a sense of joy to yield
To the bare trees, and mountains bare,
And grass in the green field.

My sister! ('tis a wish of mine)
Now that our morning meal is done,
Make haste, your morning task resign;
Come forth and feel the sun.

Edward will come with you – and, pray,
Put on with speed your woodland dress;
And bring no book: for this one day
We'll give to idleness.

This lovely poem should be used as a theme for my special project, WILD. This stands for World Idleness Day. It's a gag but should be real. We posted the following blog post on the Idler website on 1 April 2021 (geddit?):

We are thrilled to announce that today has been approved as World Idleness Day. After extensive lobbying of MPs and Lords in Parliament by the *Idler* magazine, as well as the European Union, the decision was taken to give the whole world a day off, which is great news for the idle revolution. What a lovely surprise for Easter.

Dubbed WILD, the idea of a global do-nothing day was greeted with enthusiasm by world leaders.

President of the European Commission Ursula von der Leyen said: "In these extremely challenging times we support the *Idler* magazine in its campaign to increase life-saving leisure time for all. At last the European project of wandering around in olive groves drinking wine all day begun by Socrates is being realised."

Former Governor of the Bank of England Mark Carney commented, "John Maynard Keynes foresaw that man with all his ingenuity would create a 15-hour working week by 2030. We're not there yet but WILD is a step in the right direction."

Goldman Sachs chief David Solomon, whose young staff recently complained about 100-hour working weeks, said, "We do all need to find balance in this connected world. By all means take a day off but if we all go an extra mile for our client, even when we feel that we're reaching our limit, it can really make a difference in our performance."

And Harry and Meghan commented, "We feel true, genuine compassion for all the little people out there who have to work for a living. Our hearts go out to them. We see you. For our part, we will honour Meghan and Harry Day (MAHD) by reflecting compassionately on the ills done to us by the world's media and our own struggles with mental health, wellbeing and annoying parents.'

Not all prominent Brits were in favour. Former PM David Cameron, lobbyist for collapsed usury firm Greensill, said, "Man was born to toil, to get up at six in the morning, scrape the ice off the window screen and work all the hours that God gives for a massive, cruel corporation so it can pay me millions in stock options to lobby the government to borrow money cheaply to lend to other people expensively," he said. "Idleness for me – yes – but not for the hard-working families of this country who must be kept busy in case they start thinking too much."

And former chancellor George Osborne said, "I'll be working as normal today. Hard, hard work for amoral, ruthless corporations in return for enormous wealth – that's my philosophy. None of this sitting, around-under-trees-reading-poetry nonsense."

Prime Minister Boris Johnson, however, supported WILD: "The inner idler in all of us needs as much encouragement as possible," said the UK's leader. "Otium is a jolly good thing, as Cicero taught us. And that's why I am fully behind this terrific idea. I for one will be indulging in a glorious post-prandial siesta this very day. Idle on!"

You can help by simply refusing to work today. Lie on the grass and stare at the sky instead. You'll be soothing your soul and saving the planet all in one.

You'll also be contributing to the great project conceived in the 1930s by the super-brains of the day, people like Bertrand Russell and Maynard Keynes, both of whom believed that progress should mean less work, not more.

The future mapped out by Keynes and Bertrand Russell was a life of leisure, for men and for women (and everyone in between). In his essay *Economic Possibilities for our Grandchildren*, Keynes quotes a well-known charwoman's epitaph:

> *Don't mourn for me, friends, don't weep for me never,*
> *For I'm going to do nothing for ever and ever.*

Death, then, was the only release from a life of hard toil. But Keynes thinks that mankind, with all its cleverness, should create much more time for doing nothing before death. But, he says, we're actually afraid of idling:

> [W]e have been trained too long to strive and not to enjoy. It is a fearful problem for the ordinary person, with no special talents, to occupy himself, especially if he no longer has roots in the soil or in custom or in the beloved conventions of a traditional society. To judge from the behaviour and the achievements of the wealthy classes today in any quarter of the world, the outlook is very depressing!

That's because psychopathic rich people spend their time dashing about and boasting about how busy they are, thus setting a bad example to the rest of us. Keynes ends his essay with a beautiful anti-capitalist vision of a society where money-lending is frowned upon and we laze about all day:

> I see us free, therefore, to return to some of the most sure and certain principles of religion and traditional virtue – that avarice is a vice, that the exaction of usury is a misdemeanour, and the love of money is detestable, that those walk most truly in the paths of virtue and sane wisdom who take least thought for the morrow. We shall once more value ends above means and prefer the good to the useful. We shall honour those who can teach us how to pluck the hour and the day virtuously and well, the delightful people who are capable of taking direct enjoyment in things, the lilies of the field, who toil not, neither do they spin.

So take a WILD, phone in sick, go the beach.

Inaction points

☞ Schedule your day off; plan it.

☞ Put an auto-reply on your email. You could even justify it with a reference to your mental health: "In order to protect my mental health, I will not be available via email or phone on 1 April."

22

Remove yourself from social media

Social media hates your soul.
Jaron Lanier

As Aldous Huxley correctly predicted, we humans have come to love our slavery, and we are slaves to social media.

Social media is a vanity-led advertising business. It extracts free labour out of us – promising "self-expression" and likes – and then sells advertising space back at us. It's a sneaky form of slavery, and even cheaper, since the new mill owners in Silicon Valley do not need to suffer the expense of buying the slaves. YouTube, Twitter, Instagram and Facebook have got the whole world videoing, photographing and writing for them – *working!* – for free. We upload vast oceans of content to their platforms in the hope of likes and thumbs-ups and being generally seen and heard. In other words, they feed our egos, we feed their bank accounts. But our vanity blinds us to the reality of this scam. Far from hating and fearing our oppressors, we love them, we thank them, we try to please them, we flatter them.

Posting on Twitter leads to all sorts of problems. People post quick remarks that they've not really reflected on properly. It's all done in a hurry. Then someone else out there, rightly or wrongly, gets offended, and stress and strain ensue. In the old days you might have written a letter. But the act of letter-writing by nature encourages deeper reflection than Twitter.

I remember when I decided to get off Twitter. I'd gone with my brother and our two daughters boating on the Thames at Oxford as a tribute to Lewis Carroll. We were drifting down the river, my brother gently pulling the oars, with the sound of the wind in the trees, and the cackle of the moorhen, when I checked my phone (I still had a smartphone then). There was a tweet from a grammarian objecting to some comment I'd made about the importance of the apostrophe. The tweet said "dangerous nonsense" or something similar. OK, it wasn't a death threat, but it still ruined the moment for me.

I'm just the kind of person who would send off a tweet at 10 in the evening, after a couple of beers, thinking I was being funny or clever, and end up offending someone. Some people may enjoy Twitter spats. Journalists often start them. Presumably they think it's good publicity. But they cause me anxiety.

I was delighted when one of my gurus, the tech pioneer Jaron Lanier, wrote a book denouncing social media. Jaron works at Microsoft as OCTOPUS, meaning Office of the

Chief Technology Officer Prime Unifying Scientist, and he's been named one of the 100 most influential people in the world by *Time* magazine.

The book is called *Ten Arguments for Deleting Your Social Media Accounts Right Now*. Please read it. He says that social media took behavioural science and used it to create an advertising-sales business. We humans are like Pavlov's dog, victims of non-stop experimentation. He says that social media should really be called BUMMER, or Behaviours of Users Modified, and Made into an Empire for Rent. And that social media is designed to make you into an asshole because, as he puts it, "the biggest assholes get the most attention". That's why people get weird and nasty on social media.

Twitter is a cesspit and Instagram is a lying factory. They used to say that the camera never lies, but the camera lies all the time. It photographs the tiniest nanosecond of reality, in the tiniest frame. There is zero context. On Instagram, which is a business selling ads to companies which want to sell you shit, you are encouraged to be in a perpetual state of excitement and to be living an amazing life. This leads to envy in others, even when they know that the Instagrammer is lying or at least revealing only a very slender slice of the truth.

The Seven Deadly Sins, as invented by medieval clerics, are pride, avarice, lust, anger, gluttony, envy and sloth. All of these (with the possible exception of sloth) are encouraged, promoted and rewarded by social media. The tech overlords stir up sin in the people, because it makes them

97

money (the way that these greedy psychopaths think of themselves as the anointed saviours of humanity makes the pill doubly hard to swallow).

Social-media users are blinded by their own vanity to this obvious truth. It surprises me that so many radical thinkers use Twitter, when you consider that Twitter is one of the best-developed white male capitalist swindles yet perpetrated on the planet.

Social media is also profoundly un-eco-friendly. I'm a fan of a magazine called *Data Centre News*. This august publication reports on developments in the data centre industry. Data centres are vast warehouses filled with buzzing computers which need to be constantly cooled by enormous fans. They are where our Tweets and updates and blogs and videos and Instagram posts go. And they use up extraordinary amounts of electricity. That's why, if Extinction Rebellion were serious, they would stop promoting themselves on YouTube and Facebook, because every Tweet you make, they'll not only be watching you, they'll be digging up more coal in order to send it to your followers.

At this point you may well say, "But the *Idler* has various social-media accounts," even if I do not have any personally. Yes, and in fact my guru Jaron is not saying everyone must quit immediately. Awareness is the thing. I am fully aware that many *Idler* readers love using Twitter and Facebook and so on, and that these platforms may be used for good. But be very wary – there are snares out there. One of the Epicurean sayings is that one step towards happiness comes when you stop caring what other people think of you. Social media encourages the opposite, it stimulates a hysterical desire to please, and gives you nothing back. If you got a pound a like, it would be a different story, of course.

Jaron also recommends removing yourself from social media for a short period to try it out – a day, a week, a month. He is right that social media wants you to be angry and unhappy because angry and unhappy people buy more stuff.

Inaction points

☞ Read *Ten Arguments* by Jaron Lanier or read his interviews at idler.co.uk.

☞ Take a week off Twitter and Instagram and monitor your mental health. It will improve.

☞ Buy some postcards and stamps. Send a postcard to a friend.

☞ For more advice on freeing yourself from the amoral tech overlords of Silicon Valley, check out the Idler Academy course How to Fix the Future with Andrew Keen.

23

Avoid travel

The soul is no traveller; the wise man stays at home.
Emerson

I DON'T KNOW about you, and of course I don't know how old you are, but I've found that there's something about being middle-aged that makes you behave, well, like a middle-aged person.

Take logistics. When young, I would sleep soundly the night before catching a 10am train. I would get up, leave the house, arrive at the station at ten to ten, catch the train and that was the end of it.

Now I start worrying a good week before the train leaves. I pore over timetables and consult various online map programmes in order to calculate how long it will take me to get to the station. I lie in bed pondering the issue of what time to arrive at the station and whether it's better to buy a coffee there or make one in the kitchen before I leave.

The night before the train leaves I pack my bag carefully, even though it's only a day trip. I place the bag near the front door so I won't forget it. I go to bed extra early and set the alarm at a time to allow myself plenty of time for breakfast and more worrying in the morning. I lie awake worrying that I will oversleep and miss the train.

The next morning the alarm goes off and I remember with horror that I have to catch a train. I get up and slightly curse the extra beer I had the night before – that was foolish. I behave with extreme grumpiness and bustling self-importance to any family member who attempts to engage me in conversation.

I arrive at the station a good 40 minutes before the train leaves and stare fixedly at the departure notices in order to spot the platform number the moment it is announced. I aim to find a carriage that will be situated near the exit at the other end, though of course this is guesswork. As the train pulls out of the station, with me in it, I feel an enormous sense of relief and indeed achievement. I have successfully caught a train! I feel like calling Victoria to say, "It's all going really well. I got to the station nice and early, and caught the train."

As for holidays, I start thinking about what to pack a good two weeks in advance. This sort of semi-fearful behaviour reminds me of *Simpsons* creator Matt Groening's remark about his parents, who would get up at 4am on the day of the holiday, in order to "get a good crack at the highway".

Could we all travel a bit less? As a naturally stay-at-home sort of person who is quite happy with a chair, a book and a beer, but who feels vaguely guilty about not travelling, I remember being delighted many years ago to discover that the word for "travel" derives from the Latin word *trepalium*, meaning a three-pronged instrument of torture. (*Trepalium* more recently has been taken up as the name of a French death metal band, and a dystopian French mini-series about a society split into two halves: the Actives and the Jobless. Must check that out.)

The French word *travail*, meaning "work", is also practically the same word. Travel, then, means work, possibly dangerous work, and work is what we idlers are trying to avoid. Travel was traditionally exhausting, fraught with troubles and worries, bandits and border guards, getting scurvy, losing all your money, your boat sinking in a storm, running out of food, getting arrested.

As Montaigne said, "How many we know who have fled the sweetness of a tranquil life in their homes, among their friends, to seek the horror of uninhabitable deserts; who have flung themselves into humiliation, degradation, and the contempt of the world, and have enjoyed these and even sought them out."

Today travel is a minefield of Passenger Locator Forms, confusing baggage requirements, irritatingly jaunty airlines, wires, chargers, adaptors, remembering to leave your knife and liquids at home and the five-day worry before leaving. That's not to mention the immense drain on fuels and the pollution that travel creates. Airbnb is the villain here. In the year before the pandemic, they spent $900,000,000 (yes, that's just under a billion) on marketing, i.e. on getting landlords to chuck out local tenants in favour of daft travellers. This had devastating effects on Naples, Florence and Venice, which turned into giant museums and were losing their genuine residents. The pandemic may or may not help these fine cities become homes and communities once again.

I suppose travel was getting quite easy at one point, in the nineties and noughties. Then came the War on Terror and we had to start undressing at the border. Then came the War on COVID which added new layers of bureaucracy. Good for the bureaucrats and busybodies, bad for the rest of us.

I do obviously concede that a trip away can provide you with some wonderful idling time, and some heat. I am not so churlish as to condemn all travellers and holidaymakers. But if you can create an everyday life that is pretty much how you want it, then what is there to escape from?

So if your trip is cancelled, that may be a reason for rejoicing. Staying at home is not only easy, it uses no energy, so if we are really serious about reducing our use of fossil fuels, we should travel less.

Remember, it's still you. The Roman Epicurean poet Lucretius made the point that in travelling, "each man flees himself", but he is still dogged by the same companion.

Inaction points
☞ Organise fewer trips.
☞ Learn to say no.
☞ Rejoice when a trip is cancelled.
☞ When travelling, pack light and do not cling to planned outcomes. Let go.

24
Loll by the fire

*I am confin'd to a narrow Closet, lolling on an arm chair,
nodding away my days over a fire, like the picture of
January in an old Salisbury Primer.*
Pope

I WAS SHOCKED to read recently that there's a movement
among ecological campaigners to ban fires.

Now although I am an ecological campaigner myself, or
like to consider myself one, and attempt to avoid polluting
the planet, there is a point at which ecological campaign-
ing turns into a sort of finger-wagging puritanism. No fun
allowed. Fun has an excessive carbon footprint. So stop it.
Stand around an electric radiator instead.

However, the pandemic led to a rise in standing around
piles of burning stuff. Sales of fire pits increased as we
sought out new ways to socialise. We were getting medieval, in a good way. There were even murmurs against that
smug product of American modernity air-conditioning. We
were told to fling windows open, get the air moving, which
of course is standard folk wisdom, the kind of thing that
Granny advised.

I am going to carry on making fires and staring at them. I believe that the ecologically sound method is to burn logs that have been thoroughly dried out. I'm also happy that by burning wood, I am helping to manage forests and woodland.

Just to throw it back in the face of the puritanical anti-fire brigade (ha ha), let me quote you a list of the benefits of burning wood, from a piece in *The Land* magazine by forestry expert Mike Gardner:

- Increase the timber quality of the forest;
- Increase the biodiversity of the forest;
- Increase the forest's resilience to climate change;
- Increase the forest's capacity to take up carbon;
- Replace fossil fuels with renewable wood fuel;
- Substitute local fuelwood for wood from further away;
- Provide truly green local employment.

This means that we can carry on making fires without guilt, and if George Monbiot tells you off or reports you to the authorities, throw that list in his face.

Wood is good. Fire is freedom.

And not only do fires make sense from a practical point of view; let us also celebrate their beauty and ability to create a space for both reflection and for merry-making. Sitting round the fire with some friends and some beer clearly satisfies some sort of ancient need in us. It's time to bring out the guitars and ukuleles, sing some songs together and generally make merry, away from jobs and bosses and commuting and debt.

The indoor fire is a great aid to reflection and idling. In the old days, January was the best time for lolling by the fire and it's a custom that Alexander Pope refers to in our epigram, which comes from a letter written in 1712, bemoaning his confinement during, I guess, the Christmas holiday, due to illness.

The "January" to which he refers was the two-faced god Janus from where the month gets its name. Janus looked back on the year just gone and ahead to the new year. He was all about calm reflection, fireside loafing and simply being idle.

Inaction points

☞ Order a load of dry logs. Burn them outdoors or indoors.

☞ Stare and wonder.

☞ Or just stick with a barbecue. A barbecue is a fire, it is socially acceptable, and is an easy way to cook – no washing-up!

Epilogue

I DO HOPE you've enjoyed the modest proposals listed in this book and can see that a more idle life is possible right here, right now.

Again and again the philosophers and poets tell us that wise people reject the siren strains of ambition, status and riches and embrace the world of freedom and leisure and tranquillity. The merchants and politicians are not wise and their lives are full of stress and trouble. (Why people persist in seeking glory and vast riches despite the repeated philosophical and religious warnings over the last three centuries against them is anyone's guess. I imagine it's a mix of fear and ego.)

We idlers seek to enjoy life, not to avoid it. To be an idle Epicurean, you do not need to bother retreating to a commune (most utopian schemes, in fact, end in disaster, because they are very closely related to tyrannies). You can be idle anywhere.

So let us all slow down, have fun, and live well.

Acknowledgements

Thanks to Victoria Hull, Virginia Ironside,
Colin Midson, Ed Jenne, James Pembroke,
Penny Phillips

HOW TO BE IDLE
THE MANIFESTO

THE RELIGION OF INDUSTRY HAS TURNED HUMAN BEINGS INTO WORK ROBOTS · THE IMPOSITION OF WORK-DISCIPLINE ON FREE-WHEELING DREAMERS ENSLAVES US ALL · JOY AND WISDOM HAVE BEEN REPLACED BY WORK AND WORRY · WE MUST DEFEND OUR RIGHT TO BE LAZY · IT IS IN OUR IDLENESS THAT WE BECOME WHO WE ARE; IT IS WHEN LAZY THAT WE ACHIEVE SELF-MASTERY · JOBS ROB OUR TIME · PRODUCTIVITY AND PROGRESS HAVE LED TO ANXIETY AND UNEASE · TECHNOLOGY IMPRISONS AS IT PROMISES TO LIBERATE · CAREERS ARE PHANTASMS · MONEY IS MIND FORG'D · WE CAN CREATE OUR OWN PARADISE · NOTHING MUST BE DONE · WITH FREEDOM COMES RESPONSIBILITY · STAY IN BED · BE GOOD TO YOURSELF · INACTION IS THE WELLSPRING OF CREATION · ART, PEOPLE, LIFE · BREAD, BACON, BEER · LIVE FIRST, WORK LATER · TIME IS NOT MONEY · STOP SPENDING · QUIT YOUR JOB · STUDY THE ART OF LIVING · LIVE SLOW, DIE OLD · EMBRACE NOTHING · KNOW NOTHING · DO NOTHING · BE IDLE!

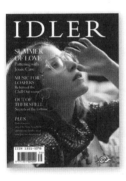

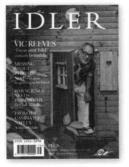
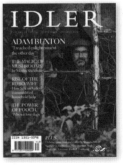

DOWN WITH SILICON VALLEY
BAKE BREAD PLAY THE UKULELE
OPEN THE VILLAGE HALL
Action IS futile Quit moaning MAKE MUSIC
STOP CONSUMING START PRODUCING
BACK TO THE LAND
SMASH USURY EMBRACE BEAUTY EMBRACE POVERTY
HAIL THE CHISEL
IGNORE the STATE REFORM IS FUTILE
ANARCHY IN THE UK
HAIL THE SPADE
HAIL THE HORSE HAIL THE QUILL
LOVE THY NEIGHBOUR
BE CREATIVE
FREE YOUR SPIRIT
DIG THE EARTH
MAKE COMPOST
LIFE IS ABSURD
WE ARE FREE
BE MERRY

Join the
Idler Mailing List

and receive *Idler* editor
Tom Hodgkinson's weekly newsletter.
You'll be the first to hear about events,
offers and our "A Drink With the
Idler" weekly gatherings, where you
can join Tom and guests for an hour
of good conversation and philosophy.

idler.co.uk/newsletter-sign-up/

SLOW DOWN
HAVE FUN
LIVE WELL